DEPARTMENT OF DEFENSE
DEFENSE SCIENCE BOARD

TASK FORCE REPORT:
Predicting Violent Behavior

August 2012

OFFICE OF THE UNDER SECRETARY OF DEFENSE FOR ACQUISITION, TECHNOLOGY AND LOGISTICS
WASHINGTON, D.C. 20301-3140

**DEFENSE SCIENCE
BOARD**

OFFICE OF THE SECRETARY OF DEFENSE
3140 DEFENSE PENTAGON
WASHINGTON, DC 20301–3140

21 August 2012

MEMORANDUM FOR UNDER SECRETARY OF DEFENSE FOR ACQUISITION,
TECHNOLOGY AND LOGISTICS

SUBJECT: Final Report of the Defense Science Board (DSB) Task Force on Predicting Violent
Behavior

I am pleased to forward the final report of the DSB Task Force on Predicting Violent
Behavior. The Task Force examined a set of issues relating to violent behavior within the DoD
community, many stemming directly from the tragic Ft. Hood shooting on 5 November 2009.

The report provides insightful recommendations for the Department against perpetrators
of "targeted violence" – those individuals who conduct pre-meditated attacks against specific
individuals, populations, or facilities. While the Task Force charter focused on *predicting* violent
behavior, they determined the most effective means of responding to the challenge of targeted
violence is to undertake *prevention* measures. To that end, the Task Force recommends a near
term focus on threat management units (TMUs) to provide an effective, low-footprint means of
mitigating threats of targeted violence in the DoD community. Key to the successful functioning
of TMUs, information sharing between concerned parties must be improved to include providing
better clarity on such sensitive issues as religious freedom, medical and legal privacy issues. In
the long term, the Task Force believes advanced science and technology has potential to assist
threat management personnel. However most of the research is conducted outside the United
States and the Department will need to monitor and then adopt relevant areas for its own use.

I endorse the Task Force's findings and recommendations and encourage you to forward
the report to the Secretary of Defense.

Dr. Paul Kaminski
Chairman

OFFICE OF THE SECRETARY OF DEFENSE
3140 DEFENSE PENTAGON
WASHINGTON, DC 20301–3140

DEFENSE SCIENCE
BOARD

14 August 2012

MEMORANDUM FOR CHAIRMAN, DEFENSE SCIENCE BOARD

SUBJECT: Final Report of the Defense Science Board (DSB) Task Force on Predicting Violent
Behavior

Attached is the final report of the DSB Task Force on Predicting Violent Behavior.
Chartered as one of several DoD efforts initiated in the wake of the 5 November 2009 Ft. Hood
shooting, the Task Force focused its efforts on individuals possessing access to military facilities
or personnel that pose a threat of "targeted violence". Individuals engaged in "targeted violence"
consider, plan and prepare before engaging in acts of violence against specific individuals,
populations, or facilities with perpetrators engaging in behaviors that precede and are related to
their attacks. Targeted violence motivators are not limited to a single cause (e.g. a particular
religious, financial, racial, or social outlook).

The Task Force developed findings and recommendations which are summarized as
follows:

There is no panacea for stopping all targeted violence. Attempting to balance risks,
benefits, and costs, the Task Force found that *prevention* as opposed to *prediction* should
be the Department's goal. Good options exist in the near-term for mitigating violence by
intervening in the progression from violent ideation to violent behavior.

**In the near-term, professional threat management, as practiced by law-
enforcement-led threat management units (TMUs) offer effective means to help
prevent targeted violence.** These units are widely deployed, with operational success, in
the private sector, academia, and elsewhere in government – but not widely across DoD.
The Department must implement threat management standards of practice, with an
emphasis on low-footprint, high-impact TMUs that largely utilize existing resources.

**Improved information sharing, recognizing the need for privacy and free religious
practice, is a vital enabler of effective threat management.** There is currently a lack of
clarity and understanding among commanders, supervisors, and healthcare providers
regarding Privacy Act and HIPAA regulations on the releasability of information that
may be relevant to documenting and reporting concerning behavior. There is a similar
lack of clarity regarding religious accommodation and what religious or protest activities
are, or are not, subject to scrutiny by commanders and supervisors. The Department,
should take action to provide a more concise, thorough understanding of actual (as
opposed to perceived) limitations on the sharing of information. In addition, DoD's
current threat information sharing architecture continues to have gaps that should be
addressed through such steps as developing a collaborative DoD-wide investigative
database, with benchmarks to assess progress

Science and technology (S&T) initiatives aimed at preventing targeted violence do show some promise over the long-term, as an aid to threat management. In the near-term, the Department should focus S&T efforts on conducting rigorous case studies to aid in the identification of valid behavioral indicators for use by trained threat management professionals. Implementing and evaluating the effectiveness of resilience training should also be a key S&T milestone in the near-term. Over the long-term, screening technologies related to biomarkers show promise and warrant close observation by the Department. This is particularly the case regarding research conducted outside the United States.

In closing, we would like to express our sincere gratitude to those from government, academia, and the private sector who briefed the Task Force over the past year. Their knowledge and experience greatly enhanced the quality of our study and played a key role in shaping our recommendations to the Department of Defense.

Mr. V. Larry Lynn
Co-Chair

Hon. Judith A. Miller
Co-Chair

Table of Contents

List of Tables and Figures

1.0 Executive Summary

1.1 Introduction

This report conveys the findings and recommendations of the Defense Science Board (DSB) Task Force (TF) on Predicting Violent Behavior. This study was chartered and co-sponsored by the Under Secretary of Defense for Acquisition, Technology, and Logistics (USD(AT&L)) and the Under Secretary of Defense for Policy (USD(P)).

This DSB study is one of several reviews that resulted from the killings that took place on November 5, 2009 at the Fort Hood, Texas Soldier Readiness Center, and is submitted in response to the Terms of Reference (TOR) of May 21, 2011. A copy of the TOR is provided in Appendix 1 to this report and summarized in Table 1 below. Task 8 was added later as a result of the Fort Hood Independent Review Panel.

1.2 Terms of Reference and Task Force Membership

The DSB Task Force members listed in Appendix 2 are a multi-disciplinary team of thought leaders and subject matter experts in law enforcement, neuroscience, engineering, medicine, forensic psychology, threat management, military and law.

Table 1. Summary of the Terms of Reference

1. Examine and evaluate existing screening programs to include those used in other branches of government, private industry, and academia for successful programs and best practices.
2. Assess the adequacy of suitability criteria conducted in periodic checks and those provided to co-workers and supervisors.
3. Evaluate the impact of the Privacy Act of 1974 and the Health Insurance Portability and Accountability Act (HIPAA), which prevent or inhibit real or perceived access to the official personnel or medical records of DoD members.
4. Assess the network requirements and information flow, which could be used to correlate information across disparate sources, organizations, time frames, and geographic locations.
5. Evaluate an organizational construct within DoD to maximize effectiveness of current and future criminal and behavioral analysis and risk assessment capabilities and tools focused on an internal threat regardless of the target.
6. Provide recommendations on best capabilities and tools for commanders/supervisors as the result of the assessment.
7. Assess existing training and education programs to better assist DoD personnel in identifying potential aberrant behavior of violent actors.

8	Focus on indicators leading to a wide range of destructive events such as workplace violence, terrorism and suicide.

1.3   Overall Conclusions

The overall conclusions of the Task Force are the following:

- Mass-casualty attacks are high consequence but very low-incidence.
  - However, *threats* of targeted violence are relatively numerous.
- There is no silver bullet to stop ALL targeted violence.
  - There is no effective formula for predicting violent behavior with any degree of accuracy.
- PREVENTION should be the goal rather than PREDICTION.
  - Good options exist in the near-term for mitigating targeted violence by intervening in the progression from violent ideation to violent behavior and by creating contexts that minimize alienation or isolation.
- In the near-term, professional threat management as practiced by law enforcement-led Threat Management Units (TMUs) offer effective means to help prevent targeted violence.
  - TMUs have been widely deployed, with operational success in the private sector, academia, and elsewhere in government – but not across the Department of Defense (with the exception of the Navy Criminal Investigative Service (NCIS)).
  - The Department of Defense (DoD) must implement threat management standards of practice, with an emphasis on low footprint, high impact TMUs that largely utilize existing resources.
- Improved information sharing – considering appropriate accommodation for privacy and free religious practice – is a vital enabler of effective threat management.
- Science and Technology (S&T) shows some promise as an aid to threat management.
  - Near-term S&T efforts should focus on conducting rigorous case studies and instituting resilience training.
  - These case studies should include clinical medical, psychological and behavioral indicators as research better defines their relevance and precision.
  - Over the long-term, screening technology related to biomarkers has potential.

1.4   Targeted Violence

Throughout this study, several experts suggested a commonality across many perpetrators of targeted violence. The Task Force defined "targeted violence" as pre-meditated attacks against specific individuals, populations, or facilities with perpetrators engaged in behaviors that precede and are related to their attacks. Perpetrators of targeted violence consider, plan, and prepare before engaging in acts of violence. Planning and preparation steps are often detectable, providing an opportunity for disruption of the intended violence. These perpetrators feel that they are not valued/validated and are singled out. They subsequently feel that organizations or specific people are out to get them. There is a shift from self-defense to self-preservation and thus a need to destroy the individuals, populations, or the organizational representatives that they feel wants to destroy them. Violence is then viewed as an option and the progression from ideation to attack begins. Targeted violence motivators are not limited to a single cause (e.g. a particular religious, financial, racial, or social outlook).

1.5 Task Force Goals

The broad mission of this TF was to develop strategies and guidelines to enhance the ability of the Department of Defense to identify and intervene with individuals linked to military facilities or personnel that may pose a threat within the work environment. Despite the prevalence of formal and informal screening mechanisms encountered throughout a person's interactions with DoD, a small number of individuals do engage in harmful behaviors, either to themselves or to others in the community. While relatively rare, these low-incidence events are often high-consequence, as exemplified by the tragic shooting at Ft. Hood on 5 November 2009 that resulted in the death of 13 people. The less quantifiable effects on the national psyche are potentially even more damaging.

Considering this mission, the TF concentrated its efforts on preventing incidents of "targeted violence" in an effective and efficient way, namely through the use of threat management techniques The Task Force also balanced individual needs (e.g. privacy, religious freedom) against the good order and discipline required to accomplish DoD's mission.

Preventing targeted violence in the DoD community requires interaction among numerous entities both inside and outside DoD (e.g. law enforcement, intelligence community, medical and legal professionals to name a few). Although there is currently no organizational construct that is focused on threat management across the DoD there is considerable overlap between preventing targeted violence and identifying or mitigating other harmful behavior such as suicide, domestic violence, sexual harassment as well as financial or emotional stress or mental illness, and counter-intelligence. Finally, advancements in science and technology may offer additional tools in this endeavor.

1.6 Current Situation

Where does the DoD stand today?

- No DoD-wide standardized process for reporting, analyzing, training, and mitigating threats of targeted violence. Only a single Threat Management Unit exists (in the Department of the Navy - NCIS).
    - Commanders and supervisors are held accountable for incidents of targeted violence that occur on their watch, but there is no framework in place to respond to red flags.
    - This is in sharp contrast to numerous public and private entities in the U.S. and internationally that currently utilize threat management practices (e.g. U.S. Postal Service, U.S. Capitol Police, Intel Corporation, Virginia Tech).

- National level information sharing: Threat information management and sharing between the DoD and the Federal Bureau of Investigation (FBI) is improving with the signing of the most recent FBI/DoD Memorandum of Understanding (MOU) and Annexes — but more remains to be done.

- Military Department level information sharing practices at the Installation/Organizational level are not sufficient to document behaviors exhibited by personnel transferring from one assignment to another.
  - There is a lack of clarity among commanders/supervisors and health-care providers, regarding access to/release of information that may be relevant to preventing targeted violence or documenting behaviors of concern. Legal access is often authorized but policy is unclear to users.

- Insufficient foundation of case studies and tools to assess relevance of behavioral risk factors, the efficacy of resilience training, and the future utility of biomarkers.

1.7   Prevention Rather Than Prediction

An important conclusion of this study is that rather than a prediction strategy (as called for in the Terms of Reference), a prevention strategy that includes an element of prediction capability but does not depend on it, can be much more effective. In the near term, behavioral observation coupled with appropriate follow-through by a team of professionals able to contextually evaluate the observations is a feasible approach. Additionally, most of the recommendations resulting from a prevention strategy are applicable in dealing with other harmful behaviors. In the longer term advances in science may produce results that will improve screening and entrance performance but the state of the art in physiological and neurological sciences today does not provide useful capability (e.g. accuracy, accessibility, etc) for predicting targeted violence. Finally, in responding to violent incidents, it is also important to balance risks, benefits and costs, not just resource costs but, for example, intrusion or privacy costs. No expenditure of resources will deter or stop all attacks.

1.8   Recommended Strategy

The recommended prevention strategy includes three components:

- Provide effective intervention capabilities throughout DoD using a threat management approach.
  - Increase likelihood of early detection and warning of problems to commanders, supervisors, co-workers with improved information sharing and knowledge.
  - Enhance awareness of the risk of targeted violence throughout DoD.

- Address information sharing restrictions.

- Employ advancements in behavioral sciences, data mining, and monitor research in the neurosciences and genomics.

1.8.1   Threat Management Approaches – Near Term

While the Task Force charter focuses on *predicting* violent behavior, the most effective means of responding to the challenge of targeted violence is to undertake *prevention* measures. For example, altering the environment or constructive interactions may prevent violence before it occurs. The ability to alter the environment or constructively intervene as a preventative measure is not inherent to one organizational construct or management practice. However, the Task Force believes a threat management approach employing multidisciplinary professionals in support of local command/supervisors provides the best practical solution. Unfortunately, DoD organizations and agencies have stove-piped policies and procedures to identify and respond to indicators of violence, which inhibit a holistic approach to address the problem of targeted violence. TMUs and threat management programs, based on tested best practices, provide a solid foundation for reducing targeted violence throughout the DoD community. The TF reviewed several programs with generally acknowledged best practices (e.g. US Postal Service, Virginia Tech, Intel Corporation, etc.) that could easily be molded to serve the DoD environment. The TMU approach does not "guarantee" elimination of instances of "targeted violence" but the Task Force found no other mechanism that provided significantly more capability without excessive cost.

A TMU is a resource for the commander/supervisor for addressing targeted violence. The TMUs mission is to prevent targeted violence by developing calculated responses to troubling behavior. The TMU is a cross-functional, multi-disciplinary team approach to assist in assessing threatening situations and developing threat abatement plans that minimize the potential risk of violence. Team members will variously have professional competence in law enforcement; risk assessment; clinical medical and psychological expertise; and social and behavioral training. TMUs are not resource intensive. The NCIS TMU consists of three full-time NCIS Special Agents, two part time analysts, and one NCIS Staff Psychologist, all located in NCIS headquarters. Additionally, there are 70 trained NCIS Special Agents and investigators who work TMU issues as a collateral duty in the field.

The challenges of threat management approaches include: observing and reporting at all command levels; overcoming the stigma of self-admission and/or peer reporting; continuing leadership attention; establishing a culture of support; limitations on information sharing; and developing a reporting process that facilitates getting the information about a potential threat to the correct actors with the right resources. Commanders and supervisors face a multitude of problems and issues each and every day. Some issues can be handled with well-resourced and clearly identified processes. Other issues involve ad hoc or ill-defined processes. Institutionally, no standardized process in the Department exists for commanders and supervisors to be able to identify and track individuals that have been seen or reported to exhibit behaviors deemed potentially violent and detrimental, and that facilitate information to the right resources for screening and assessment. The Threat Management Unit provides both a resource and process focus for both commanders and supervisors.

Commanders and supervisors must be trained on how to better identify threats, intervene when necessary, and apply appropriate resources to mitigate or prevent an attack. They must possess ready access to trained professionals to fulfill their responsibilities.

An individual's coworkers are likely to be the most sensitive sensors of aberrant or troubling behavior. Training and the establishment of a trusted and transparent system for reporting such observations are essential enablers.

There is considerable overlap between predicting/preventing violence and dealing with other harmful behaviors such as suicide, sexual harassment, difficulties coping with financial or medical stress, and reduced resilience. Combining these in one support structure offers advantages and sharing of critical resources (e.g. trained personnel).

1.8.1.1 The Role of Behavioral Indicators

In the immediate aftermath of the Fort Hood shootings, the Department focused on a goal of trying to develop lists of behavioral indicators for wide use. Until such lists were developed, the Department's interim guidance was to use the behavioral indicators founds in the adjudicative guidelines for granting security clearances. The Task Force found little to no relationship between the adjudicative guidelines and targeted violence. The Task Force also found that indicator lists are most effective in the hands of trained professionals and are not an effective substitute for a more nuanced, comprehensive set of factors developed by threat-management practitioners. If not handled properly and by trained personnel, lists can lead to high false-positives with accompanying stigma, lack of trust, and reluctance to report. Lists also tend to be static and unless continually revisited the list of indicators becomes less likely to identify adaptive perpetrators who will purposefully avoid elements of listed behavior to avoid interdiction. Later in the report the Task Force discusses and recommends building a case file of DoD-related targeted violence events which is likely to provide factors for threat management practitioners and may be used to inform generalized training and information campaigns similar to suicide awareness campaigns.

Instead of relying on a list of behavioral indicators, the Task Force instead recommends (as part of an integrated threat management training and communication program) that training of co-workers and other observers focus on typical questions that serve to triage initial reports of aberrant behavior : (1) Has there been any mention of suicidal thoughts, plans, or attempts? (2) Has there been any mention of thoughts or plans of violence? (3) Have there been any behaviors that cause concern for violence or the person's well being? (4) Does the person have access or are they trying to gain contextually inappropriate access to a weapon? (5) Are there behaviors that are significantly disruptive to the workplace environment? Reports then can be made to threat management professionals for evaluation and appropriate follow-up. (An expanded list of 11 key questions, as used by the U.S. Secret Service is in Appendix 8.)

1.8.1.2 Threat Management Near Term Recommendations

The Secretary of Defense direct a Department-wide requirement for the Military Departments and DoD Agencies to establish a multidisciplinary TMU that identifies, assesses, and responds/manages threats of targeted violence.

- Designate an Executive Agent (EA) responsible for overseeing and managing the Department's TMUs. The EA would be responsible for management, oversight, identifying resources and training requirements, and serve as DoD's central point for threat management – with OSD policy oversight.

- Charter the Executive Agent to conduct operationally relevant research on the nature and extent of targeted violence affecting the DoD community in order to inform the operation of TMUs.

The designated Executive Agent should establish effective information sharing and communications among DoD TMUs and with appropriate non-DoD organizations:

- Establish an information sharing system that would facilitate the review and assessment of communications or behaviors of concern for immediate use by the TMUs and for analytic purposes.

- Develop and implement a communication strategy to establish a higher level of awareness regarding the risk of targeted violence throughout DoD. This should include methods of messaging to the DoD community and establishing multimodal response channels to optimize the capture of critical threat reports.

- Efforts dealing with targeted violence should take advantage of the significant overlap and be integrated as appropriate with related efforts including suicide prevention, impulsive violence, sexual harassment, early warning signs of Post-Traumatic Stress Disorder (PTSD), and coping with medical or financial stress, particularly with respect to the professional resources involved and associated training programs.

1.8.2 Information Sharing Limitations

1.8.2.1 Privacy and Religious Accommodation Issues

This section deals with real and perceived privacy and Health Insurance Portability and Accountability Act (HIPAA) limitations, and religious and legal constraints. The Task Force learned that in many cases in which service members engaged in acts of targeted violence, information was available prior to the violent act indicating that the individual demonstrated one or more of the following:

- contemplated harming himself or others;
- was in need of help due to stressful life circumstances;
- was otherwise isolated from his colleagues, depressed, or engaged in questionable associations or activities.

Relevant information might have been known to co-workers, family members or neighbors, even supervisors and commanders. In some cases relevant information was known to medical or law enforcement personnel. In many instances the information was ignored, suppressed or otherwise failed to result in diversion, intervention, or effective help being provided to the individual prior to the violent act. Strands of information may be of dubious relevancy in isolation but when shared, compiled, and analyzed by professionals may present a compelling case for intervention. Likewise, specific information indicating that a violent act may be imminent needs to be expeditiously transmitted to authorities in a position to prevent the act.

Improved sharing of information while clearly useful as a tool in detecting and preventing potential targeted violence also presents the risk of intrusive and offensive encroachment on personal privacy. In our society personal privacy is generally a cherished cultural value. The tension between protection of personal privacy and other important public policy objectives has broad implications. This includes statutory law and even has a Constitutional dimension. Two statutes are particularly pertinent: the Privacy Act and the Privacy Rule of HIPAA. In addition the Constitution protects religious freedom.

There is a lack of clarity and understanding – among both Commanders/Supervisors and healthcare providers – regarding Privacy Act and HIPAA regulations on the releasability of information that may be relevant to documenting and reporting concerning behavior. This lack of understanding leads to an abundance of caution and impedes information flow. The default behavior is to not release any information that could potentially fall under the Privacy Act or HIPAA.

There is a similar lack of clarity and understanding regarding religious accommodation. The fact that the free exercise of religion is a Constitutional right and that DoD policy favors accommodation of religious practices in no way protects activities that may be evidence of an intent to commit violent acts, otherwise harm others, or disrupt the military mission. Such activities even though clothed in religious terminology or undertaken in a religious context are not immunized from scrutiny and appropriate action.

This lack of clarity can be addressed by the DoD General Counsel (DoD GC) and Privacy office collaboratively preparing concise guidance on the Privacy Act and HIPAA (and if necessary, considering new regulations or legislation), and revision of policy guidance to state *expressly* that religious speech or activity of a violent extremist nature is not immunized from scrutiny merely by association with religious rhetoric or belief.

1.8.2.2 Information Sharing Limitations--Organizational

During the course of its work, the Task Force encountered some information sharing limitations originating from organizational construct and practices. The Task Force reviewed two additional Ft Hood related tasks identified as potential gaps in the Final Review. (1) Commanders/Supervisors do not have sufficient visibility into the personnel records of those transferring into their command/office. Each new assignment effectively represents a "clean slate" whereby behaviors of concern are not documented across assignments, patterns get lost, and prevention becomes significantly more difficult. (2) Opportunities may exist for continued improvements in communications between DoD and federal law enforcement with regard to sharing of threat information, particularly with regard to operational behavioral threat assessments and threat management strategies.

The Task Force also found that the Military Departments, with the exception of the Department of the Army, currently operate a centralized, combined intelligence, counter intelligence and law enforcement threat information sharing capability. The Task Force felt that the separation of these key entities in any organization perpetuates failure and significantly limits an organization's ability to accurately access the nature of any type of threat. The current relationship between the U.S. Army Intelligence and Security Command (INSCOM), the U.S. Army Criminal Investigation Command (CID), and law enforcement should be revaluated with the goal of operating in a more integrated manner without inserting organizational boundaries as potential barriers to the rapid flow of relevant information.

The body of this report and its appendices detail specific legal language that represents limitations on relevant information sharing. However, the Task Force concluded that current law and accepted practice do not in fact unduly restrict information flow—if implemented properly.

1.8.2.3 Information Sharing Recommendations

A. The General Counsel, collaboratively with other elements of the Department, develop clear and comprehensible guidance to provide better understanding to supervisors/commanders of actual (as opposed to perceived) limitations on sharing of information:

- 1. Review the impact of privacy rules including those under the Privacy Act and HIPAA. If adverse impacts to the necessary flow of information are found, DoD should (1) take steps to mitigate those impacts, and, if found necessary (2) advance corrective legislative proposals.

- 2. DoD guidance (such as DoDI 1325.06, Handling Dissident and Protest Activity Among Military Members) should expressly state that religious speech or activities of a radical nature detrimental to DoD policy on conduct and behavior are not immunized from scrutiny merely by association with religious rhetoric or belief.

- 3. Prepare concise, easily understood guidance on privacy and religious rules as they affect personnel actions and exchange of information on matters discussed in this report.

B. The Under Secretary of Defense for Intelligence and the Under Secretary of Defense for Policy, in coordination with the FBI, reassess DoD's current threat information sharing architecture both internal to the Department and externally with the goal of evaluating the migration of threat information down to the user level in a timely and thorough manner.

- 1. As part of the assessment, DoD in collaboration with the FBI should develop a comprehensive, DoD-wide investigative database that would serve as a central repository of threat information. The database should be a collaborative endeavor ensuring all threat information is discoverable and accessible to trained threat management professionals experienced in sharing threat information with commanders and supervisors.

■ 2. Design a system of bench marks and metrics to be used to monitor and provide feedback from senior officials down to the user level on the effectiveness of information sharing practices and programs internal to the Department and with external partners.

C. The Department of the Army evaluate the organizational barriers that exist between INSCOM, CID and law enforcement and provide metrics to support current organizational constructs or develop new organizational constructs to improve the information flow.

1.8.3   Science and Technology

Neuroscience, genetics, and behavioral relationships are very active areas of research. The Task Force conducted an exhaustive inquiry into current tools including various prediction systems, none of which withstood intense scrutiny on reliability, practicality, and maturity. While there are promising indicators that might predict aberrant behavior, severe personality disorders, addiction, and other anti-social behaviors, the current state of the science is such that the false positives and false negatives are very high. In addition, developing a practical means to observe any useful indicators may present a significant challenge.

Nevertheless, the existing biomarker/behavioral field represent an important near term area for research into the determinants of violence, and may have long-term applications in identification and prediction. Consequently, DoD should monitor the ongoing research in these and other related areas.

In the near-term the S&T community should conduct in-depth case studies to inform assessment of behavioral risk factors, evaluate Army merger of personnel databases (trend analysis, data correlations), assess outcome of resiliency training, and initiate physiological biomarker-based measurement program. The overall goal would be to quantify the variance in the performance of individuals.

1.8.3.1 Recommendations for Science and Technology

Assistant Secretary of Defense (Research and Engineering) (ASD(R&E) should undertake a unified, but modest, effort to understand and test the performance of emerging tools, building on promising starts within and outside the DoD.

- ■ In the near term, focus on conducting cases studies, resiliency training, and analyzing physiological biomarkers.
  - ○ Collect and analyze behavioral science data in two domains:
    - ▪ Case studies of violent behavior – integrate behavioral indicators into implementation of TMU.
    - ▪ Follow and evaluate the Army's merger of personnel databases (initiated by the Army's Research and Analysis Facilitation Team (RAFT)); conduct trend and impact analysis.

- o Augment resilience training by identifying factors to improve effectiveness and specificity of training to enhance inherent adaptability.
    - Build on the Army's Comprehensive Soldier Fitness (CSF) program.
- o Biomarkers
    - Initiate biomarker-based measurement program to add "hard data," e.g. physiological measures, to the stress resiliency database.
    - Correlate physiological measurements with environmental factors to assess resiliency in the field.
    - Develop available rugged, miniaturized rapid diagnostics for battalion level use.
- Long-term: Biomarker Research and Development.
    - o Monitor international research in the neurosciences and genomics as they relate to violent behavior.

1.9   Conclusions

- Prevention should be the goal, not prediction.
- No approach should be expected to be 100%.
- Focus on TMUs will be the most effective prevention mechanism.
- Eliminate information sharing restrictions
    - o Clarify and articulate boundaries between privacy, religion, and good order and discipline
    - o Evaluate interdepartmental information processes from provider to end user with a focus on enabling work at the local level and not on administrative process at headquarter level
    - o Evaluate intra agency information processing within the Department of the Army.
- Screening techniques are immature, but scientific advances warrant watching and modest internal investments.

2.0 Introduction

2.1   Background and Context

Following the tragic mass shooting at the Fort Hood Soldier Readiness Center on 5 November 2009, then-Secretary of Defense Robert M. Gates established the Department of Defense Independent Review Related to Fort Hood, led by Admiral Vern Clark, U.S. Navy (Ret), and the Honorable Togo West. Two months after an attack that claimed thirteen lives and wounded forty-three others, the Independent Review Panel issued its report, *Protecting the Force: Lessons from Fort Hood.*[1]

The findings and recommendations of the Independent Review Panel addressed four key issue areas relevant to preventing future mass-casualty attacks within the DoD community, including personnel policies, force protection procedures, emergency response plans, and mental health care support. Significantly, the panel's findings provided an overarching framework to guide numerous follow-on studies, reviews, and assessments conducted in the wake of the Fort Hood tragedy.

Chartered in May 2011 by the Under Secretary of Defense for Acquisition, Technology, and Logistics (USD(AT&L)), and the Undersecretary of Defense for Policy (USD(P)) the Defense Science Board (DSB) Task Force on Predicting Violent Behavior is part of this ongoing effort to identify and implement lessons-learned from the Fort Hood attack. The Terms of Reference (TOR) provided to the DSB included seven specific items for the Task Force to address:

- Examine and evaluate existing screening programs to include those used in other branches of government, private industry, and academia for successful programs and standards of practice.
- Assess the adequacy of suitability criteria conducted in periodic checks and those provided to co-workers and supervisors.
- Evaluate the impact of the Privacy Act of 1974 and the Health Insurance Portability and Accountability Act (HIPAA), which prevent or inhibit real or perceived access to the official personnel or medical records of DoD members.
- Assess the network requirements and information flow, which could be used to correlate information across disparate sources, organizations, time frames, and geographic locations.
- Evaluate an organizational construct within DoD to maximize effectiveness of current and future criminal and behavioral analysis and risk assessment capabilities and tools focused on an internal threat regardless of the target.
- Provide recommendations on best capabilities and tools for commanders/supervisors as the result of the assessment.

---

[1] *Protecting the Force: Lessons from Fort Hood.* Report of the DoD Independent Review (Arlington, VA: Department of Defense, January 2010).

■ Assess existing training and education programs to better assist DoD personnel in identifying potential aberrant behavior of violent actors.

In addition to these seven tasks, the TOR directed the Task Force to "focus on observable behavior that can be identified during a periodic check or in daily interaction; and investigate the potential applicability and efficacy of cyber behavior...The Task Force should focus on the indicators leading to a wide range of destructive events, such as workplace violence, terrorism, and suicide."

2.2   Refining Scope and Focusing Questions

In response to the tasking contained in the TOR and subsequent memoranda from senior DoD leadership, the Task Force began its inquiry in April 2011. During the early information gathering stages of the study, Task Force participants refined the scope of the study, seeking to achieve three goals: (1) an approach to reducing targeted violence that balances socio-cultural approaches with innovative science and technology initiatives; (2) properly calibrate incidence, consequences, and investment; and (3) take into account the legal, moral, and ethical concerns inherent in attempting to prevent violent behavior.

Over nine months of information gathering, the Task Force received 50+ briefings from subject matter experts in government, industry and academia.

2.3   Low Incidence/High Consequence

Tragedies like the Ft. Hood shooting are rare within the DoD community (Table 2 lists a small number of targeted violence incidents that occurred internally and externally to DoD). Nevertheless, such heinous acts are extremely high consequence – both for the families immediately impacted by the event, the broader military community, and the national psyche. Indeed, years after the attack on Fort Hood, the events of November 2009 are still a central focus of policy discussions on insider threat, and countering radicalization and violent extremism within the military.

There are no statistics that capture the magnitude of the problem in terms of human devastation but the numbers are small while the impact is enormous. The upper limit that is tabulated is "homicides" and clearly the deaths from targeted violence are a small fraction of that. Figures 1 and 2 contain 30 years of data for active duty military deaths. Homicides are a very small fraction (3-7%) of all deaths and it is obvious that targeted violence is a small fraction of homicides

While large scale tragedies like Ft. Hood are rare, threats of violent behavior occur every day in a variety of settings. For this reason, the Task Force deviates from the Terms of Reference by focusing on *prevention* as opposed to *prediction*. During the information gathering phase of the Task Force's work, it became clear that prediction – with any acceptable measure of reliability – was beyond the capability of modern science and technology. However, in contrast to predicting exceedingly rare incidents of mass targeted violence, it is possible to *prevent* occurrence of most of the numerous threats of targeted violence that are made each day from escalating to actual violence using threat management principles.

Additionally, throughout the report, the Task Force refers to targeted violence in place of violent behavior. Whereas violent behavior captures a broad spectrum of actions regardless of intent, targeted violence provides a much higher degree of specificity. Equally important, targeted violence motivators are not limited to a single cause (e.g. a particular religious, financial, racial, or social outlook). The focused specificity is particularly helpful when considering the unique role of the military, and the fact that violent behavior in the context of lawful and just orders is often a central focus of military training and operations. Targeted violence is defined by the Task Force as:

> "Acts of pre-meditated attacks against specific individuals, populations or facilities with behaviors that precede and are related to their attacks. Perpetrators consider, plan and prepare before engaging in acts of violence. These behaviors are often detectable; providing an opportunity for disruption of the intended violence by utilizing a comprehensive, multi-disciplinary approach to assessment and intervention."

The overall goal of the Defense Science Board Task Force on Predicting Violent Behavior is to develop strategies and protocols to enhance the ability of DoD to identify and intervene with individuals linked to military facilities or personnel that may impose a threat within the work environment.

Table 2. Examples of Targeted Violence

Targeted Violence	
DoD - CONUS	
Ft. Bragg sniper	October 27, 1995 / 1 Killed / 18 Wounded
Anthrax Attacks*	September 2001 / 5 Killed / 17 Infected
Ft. Dix	May 2007 / Attempted
Ft. Hood	November 5, 2009 / 13 Killed / 29 Wounded
Ft. Hood	July 28, 2011 / Attempted
Non-DoD	
University of Texas	August 1, 1966 / 16 Killed / 31 Wounded
Columbine	April 20, 1999 / 12 Killed / 21 Wounded
Virginia Tech	April 16, 2007 / 32 Killed / 27 Wounded

*Although none of the victims of the anthrax attacks were DoD employees, the alleged perpetrator accessed the anthrax at a military facility. Additionally, the perpetrator selectively mailed envelopes vice conducted an aerial dispersion of the anthrax.

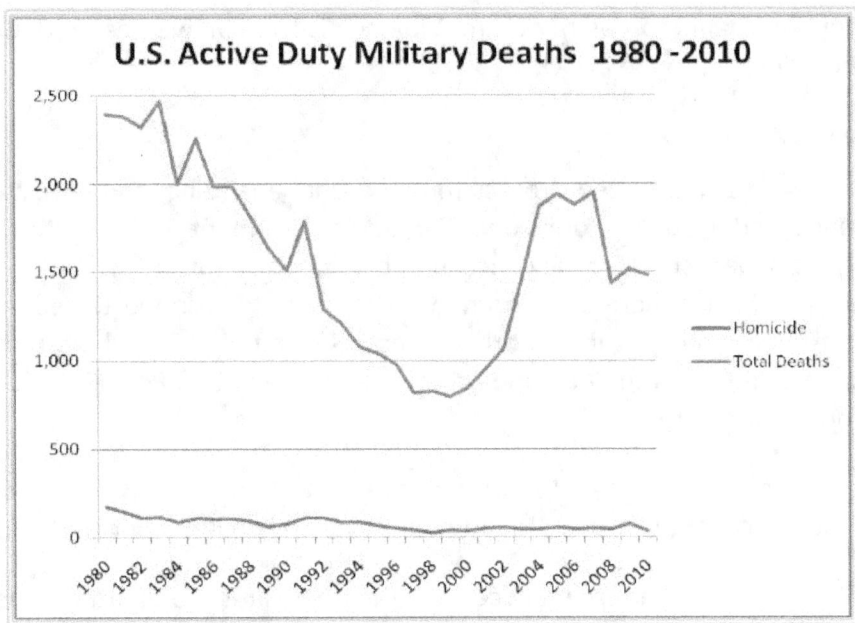

Figure 1. U.S. Active Duty Military Deaths 1980-2010[2]

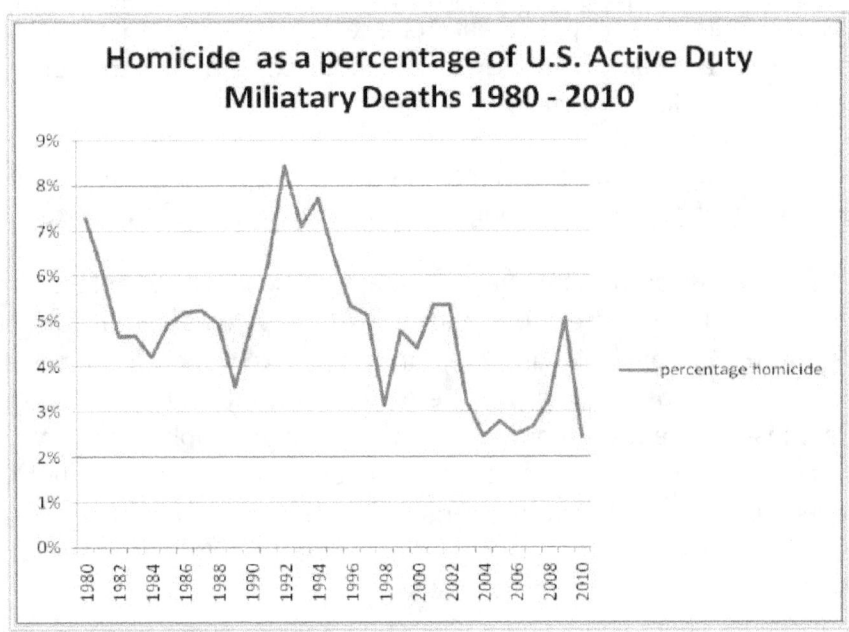

Figure 2. Homicide as a percentage of U.S. Active Duty Deaths 1980-2010[3]

The individuals or groups that perpetrate targeted violence often have mental states that in some ways are or can be quite similar. Typically they feel that they are not valued or validated and are singled out. They subsequently feel that organizations or people are out to get them and this leads to a shift from self-defense to self-preservation and thus a need to destroy the

---

[2] Department of Defense Personnel and Procurement, DoD Personnel and Military Casualty Statistics, Military Casualty Information. \http://siadapp.dmdc.osd.mil/. Internet release date: 9/30/2011.

[3] Ibid.

object that they feel wants to destroy them. Violence is then viewed as an option, beginning the progression from ideation to attack.

2.4   Where We Are Today

There is no DoD-wide standardized process for reporting, analyzing, and mitigating threats of targeted violence and DoD has only one Threat Management Unit located in the NCIS. Commanders and supervisors are held accountable for incidents of targeted violence that occurs on their watch, but there is no framework in place to respond to red flags. This is in sharp contrast to numerous public and private entities – in the U.S. and internationally - that currently utilize threat management standards of practice (e.g. U.S. Postal Service, U.S. Capitol Police, Intel Corporation, Virginia Tech).

Threat information management and sharing between DoD and the FBI is improving with the signing of the most recent FBI/DoD MOU and Annexes (Detailed in section 4.8).

Service-level information sharing practices at the installation/organization level are not sufficient to document concerning behaviors exhibited by personnel transferring from one assignment to another. There is a lack of clarity among commanders/supervisors and healthcare providers regarding access to and release of information that may be relevant to preventing incidents of targeted violence or documenting concerning behaviors; access is often authorized but policy is unclear to users.

There is an insufficient foundation of case studies and tools to assess relevance of behavioral risk factors, the efficacy of resilience training, and the future utility of biomarkers.

In the near term, professional threat management as practiced by law-enforcement-led Threat Management Units (TMU) offer effective means to help prevent targeted violence. TMUs have been widely deployed, with operational success in the private sector, academia and elsewhere in government, but not across DoD where the only significant unit is in the NCIS. DoD must implement threat management standards of practice, with an emphasis on low-footprint, high impact TMUs that largely utilize existing resources. In addition, it should be noted that there is considerable overlap between preventing targeted violence and identifying/mitigating other important behavioral issues such as suicide, domestic violence, sexual harassment, financial/emotional stress, and counter-intelligence.

Improved information sharing, taking into account the need for privacy and free religious practice, is a vital enabler of effective threat management.

Science and technology show some promise over the longer term as an aide to threat management but near term S&T efforts should focus on conducting rigorous case studies and research measures of effectiveness for resilience training. Over the long term, screening technology related to biomarkers shows some promise.

2.5   Final Report Roadmap

Chapter Three will provide analysis, findings, and recommendations addressing behavioral approaches to preventing targeted violence, followed by Chapter Four which examines information sharing and privacy in the context of the current legal and policy framework. Chapter Five focuses on science and technology approaches to understanding the underlying psychological and physiological precursors to – and correlates of – violent behavior. The recommendations of the Task Force are summarized in Chapter Six, followed by several appendices that include supplementary information relevant to the Task Force recommendations.

3.0 Behavioral Approaches: Near Term

One goal of the DSB Task Force on Predicting Violent Behavior is to recommend policies, strategies, and protocols to enhance the ability of the Department of Defense to identify and prevent targeted violence. Currently, the broader federal government, higher education, and the private sector utilize threat assessment principles to mitigate threats of targeted violence. Many of these organizations have set up formal programs with dedicated resources; however, these practices have not been widely adopted throughout the DoD. The overarching goal of this chapter is to provide guidance and recommendations to help facilitate the adoption of these proven standards of practice and program structures across the DoD community.

3.1 Targeted Violence: Prevention v. Prediction, Definition, & Common Misperceptions

Although the Terms of Reference focuses on *predicting* violent behavior, the Task Force found that the most effective means of responding to the challenge of targeted violence is to use *prevention* measures. An established threat management program, based on tested standards of practice, can provide a solid foundation for achieving a minimum-violence environment throughout the DoD community.[4]

The Task Force considered many terms and definitions during its deliberations; with the greatest focus on "targeted violence." The Task Force defined targeted violence as:

> Pre-conceived violence focused on individuals, groups, or locations where perpetrators are engaged in behaviors that precede and are related to their attacks. These perpetrators consider, plan, and prepare before engaging in acts of violence and are often detectable, providing an opportunity for disruption of the intended violence.

In determining that targeted violence was a crucial focus of its work, the Task Force also considered certain misperceptions about targeted violence that may interfere with efforts to prevent it. Those misperceptions and realities are displayed in Table 3.

---

[4] Paraphrasing USPS Threat Assessment Team Guide: "The most effective way to respond to the problem of workplace violence is to engage prevention measures. An established workplace prevention program provides the foundation for achieving a violence-free workplace."

Table 3. Misperceptions about Targeted Violence

Misperceptions about Targeted Violence:	
Misperception:	Targeted violence only involves homicide.
Reality:	Incidents of targeted violence are less about homicide and more about assaults, intimidation and fear.
Misperception:	Targeted violence occurs without warning or clues.
Reality:	Violent offenders provide a series of verbal and/or physical clues to others in the community.
Misperception:	There is no way to predict targeted violence.
Reality:	Clues to targeted violence are present, but may not be recognized or reported to members of the community who need to know.
Misperception:	People are either violent or nonviolent.
Reality:	Human behavior is variable. Those once perceived as nonviolent can and do commit violent acts.

3.2 Examples of Targeted Violence: Mass Casualty Events

Mass casualty attacks, like those listed below, are low-incidence, high-consequence events that can have a profound impact not only on the community directly affected but the nation as a whole.

1. Virginia Tech

Few events in the last decade demonstrate the catastrophic impact one person can have on a community as did the shooting at Virginia Tech University in Blacksburg, Virginia. On April 16, 2007, Seung Hui Cho, an angry and disturbed student, shot to death 32 students and faculty of Virginia Tech, wounded 17 more, and then killed himself.

2. Shooting at U.S. Postal Service processing plant

On January 30, 2006, former postal employee Jennifer San Marco shot and killed her one-time neighbor, Beverly Graham, and then drove to the mail processing plant where she had previously worked in Goleta, California. San Marco entered the facility grounds by following another car through the gate. She took an employee's identification badge at gunpoint and used the badge to enter a building, where she shot and killed six plant employees with a 9mm handgun before taking her own life.

3. Tucson shooting

At approximately 10:10 a.m. on January 8, 2011, a lone gunman approached a Safeway supermarket location in Tucson, Arizona, where U.S. Representative Gabrielle Giffords was hosting a public meeting for constituents called "Congress on Your Corner." The gunman allegedly opened fire on Giffords, as well as numerous bystanders, killing six people including Chief U.S. District Court Judge John Roll. Thirteen other people were injured by gunfire. Giffords, the apparent target of the attack, was shot in the head and left in critical condition.

3.3   Threat Assessment and Threat Management

The purpose of threat assessment is to identify potential perpetrators of targeted violence and to assess and manage the risks of such violence. The threat assessment approach is based upon three fundamental principles.[5] First, targeted violence is conceptualized as the end result of an understandable process of thinking and behaviors. The demographic and psychological characteristics central in profiling-based approaches to the identification of potential perpetrators of targeted violence are de-emphasized in favor of identifying thoughts and behaviors consistent with future violence toward an identifiable target or targets. Second, targeted violence is understood as resulting from an interaction among three distinct factors: the perpetrator of the violent act(s), a stimulus or "triggering condition" that leads the perpetrator to view violence as a solution to some problem or concern, and environmental characteristics that facilitate the violent act. Third, the planning and preparation in which the potential perpetrator engages necessarily results in discrete, observable behaviors that evince his or her intention to engage in targeted violent action. The identification of these behaviors is key to the assessment and management of potential perpetrators. In their article "Threat Assessment: An Approach to Prevent Targeted Violence" Robert Fein and colleagues address the assessment and management of potential perpetrators in greater detail.[6] The authors enumerate four important points regarding the identification of potential perpetrators of targeted violence: (a) the development of criteria that would trigger the initiation of a threat assessment investigation; (b) the identification of individuals or groups within an organization who are responsible for receiving information and conducting investigations; (c) the notification of organizations and individuals that may have direct contact with potential perpetrators that a threat assessment program is in existence, and; (d) dissemination of the criteria that would trigger a threat assessment investigation to those organizations and individuals.

With much emphasis now being placed on preventing acts of violence, rather than simply reacting to them, threat assessment activities have become a law enforcement responsibility dovetailing with community policing efforts. Consistent with available standards (e.g., the Association of Threat Assessment Professionals (ATAP), American Society for Industrial Security (ASIS)) threat assessment teams have utilized a security-driven but multidisciplinary approach utilizing behavioral health, law enforcement, human resource, and legal personnel.

The Task Force concluded that a threat assessment approach can be helpful given the multifaceted underlying motivations behind threats against the DoD. As a large employer, the Department must be mindful of the risk workplace violence poses to its vast uniformed, civilian, and contractor workforce. Further, as the nation's protector, DoD personnel can also be the target of extremist and radicalized behavior motivated by a range of religious and political motivations. Given the vast array of potential targeted violent threats faced, the delineation of

---

[5] Borum, R., Fein, R., Vossekuil, B., & Berglund, J. 1999. "Threat assessment: Defining an Approach for Evaluating Risk of Targeted Violence," *Behavioral Sciences & the Law 17(3)*: 323-337; Fein, R. A., & Vossekuil, B. 1998. "Protective Intelligence and Threat Assessment Investigations: A guide for State and Local Law Enforcement Officials," *NIJ/OJP/DOJ Publication*, no. NCJ 170612.

[6] Fein, Robert A., Vossekuil, B., Holden, G.A. 1995. "Threat Assessment: An Approach to Prevent Targeted Violence," *NIJ Research in Action* (July).

specific and all-encompassing risk factors attempting to predict such behavior would be overwhelming and potentially misleading. Instead, a behaviorally driven, structured decision-making approach based upon empirically tested approaches would be desirable. Such a threat assessment approach has been successfully applied and researched across a variety of relevant areas of targeted violence: (a) the assessment and management of targeted violence risk and problematic approach toward celebrities and high-ranking government officials, (b) the assessment and management of targeted violence risk in schools, (c) the prevention and management of workplace violence, (d) stalking, and (e) insider threat.[7]

Given the potential impact posed by extremist behavior and other forms of targeted violence, threat assessment approaches have been empirically tested to delineate risk factors discriminating between non-problematic behavior and problematic approach (including violent behavior and near-miss cases).[8] In addition, threat assessment approaches have been found effective in maximizing resources for preventing the escalation of problematic activities when applied in other governmental and educational contexts.[9]

Threat Assessment as an applied technique continues to develop and grow in the private and public sector. Changes in legislation and lobbying efforts by victim advocates have placed an increasing emphasis on the challenges of managing individuals who present threats at home, work, and to the community.

3.4   Threat Management Units

3.4.1   Description of TMUs

The focus of a TMU is to provide assessment and management of criminal and concerning behavior in matters involving targeted violence, to include workplace violence (WPV), stalking, and threatening communications. The analysis of behaviors and communications often includes interview strategies and violence risk assessments of individuals threatening violence. This often includes a multidisciplinary team comprised of law enforcement, security, forensic psychology, human resource, and legal professionals. Demand for the TMU assessments are contingent upon the policy and culture of an organization, the degree of workforce awareness, and the laws of the respective State. Additionally, in law enforcement agencies, TMUs provide investigative support in cases involving bomb threats, high risk domestic violence (DV),

---

[7]Scalora, M.J., Wells, D.G., & Zimmerman, W. 2008. "Use of Threat Assessment for the Protection of Congress," *Stalking, Threats, and Attacks Against Public Figures*, ed. J. Hoffman, J.R. Meloy, and L. Sheridan (New York: Oxford University Press); Turner, J.T., & Gelles, M.G. 2003. *Threat Assessment: A Risk Management Approach*. New York: Haworth Press); Palarea, R. E., Zona, M. A., Lane, J. C., & Langhinrichsen-Rohling, J. 1999. "The Dangerous Nature of Intimate Relationship Stalking: Threats, Violence, and Associated Risk Factors," *Behavioral Sciences and the Law* 17: 269-283; Bulling, D., Scalora, M., Borum, R., Panuzio J.; and Donica, A. 2008. "Behavioral Science Guidelines for Assessing Insider Threats" *Publications of the University of Nebraska Public Policy Center*, paper 3, http://digitalcommons.unl.edu/publicpolicypublications/37.

[8] Scalora, M.J., Zimmerman, W., & Wells, D.G. 2008. Use of Threat Assessment for the Protection of Congress. In Meloy J.R., Sheridan L, Hoffmann J. (Eds). *Stalking, Threats, and Attacks Against Public Figures*. New York: Oxford Univ. Press.

[9] James, D.V. & Warren, L. (in press) "Threat and Threats: Assessment and Management," In J. Gunn & P. Taylor (eds.) *Forensic Psychiatry 2nd ed.*(London: Hodder Arnold).

---

espionage, robbery, aggravated assault, juvenile crimes, crisis negotiations, and other violent crimes.

The current mission of TMUs is to prevent and reduce the incidence of targeted violence. It is a model that is proactive, multi-disciplinary, multi-functional, and responsive. The goals of the TMU are to identify risk factors, note patterns of behavior which may indicate escalating violence, provide investigators and security professionals with immediate analysis and assessment of threatening communications, recommendations regarding investigative strategies, and security related solutions.

TMUs that are embedded in law enforcement agencies and private industry vary in size and complexity depending on the nature of the community they are serving. Teams consist of program managers, field agents, legal counsel, and forensic psychologists. To professionalize the TMU all team members require specialized training. A current consensus amongst threat management professionals recommends that TMU team members receive a minimum of 16 hours of annual training to maintain professional standards.

3.4.2   Examples of Threat Management Units

In order to meet critical challenges and provide operationally meaningful threat assessments, numerous public, private, and academic entities have created TMUs. Figure 3 provides a non-comprehensive list of entities that maintain operating TMUs.

Department of Defense:
- NCIS

Public/Government:
- Los Angeles Police Department
- California Highway Patrol
- Los Angeles County Sheriff's Department
- Maricopa County Sheriff's Department
- San Jose Police Department
- San Diego County District Attorney's Office
- Los Angeles City Attorney's Office
- NYPD
- FBI
- US Postal Service
- CIA
- US Capitol Police
- DHS-FPS
- Veteran's Affairs OIG
- US Supreme Court
- US Secret Service
- Nebraska State Patrol
- Lincoln Police Department (Nebraska)

Higher Education:
- University of Nebraska-Lincoln
- Virginia Tech
- University of Virginia
- Iowa State University
- Pepperdine University
- University of North Carolina
- Virginia Commonwealth University
- Penn State
- Georgetown University
- University of Iowa
- Auburn University
- Georgia Tech
- Texas A&M
- George Mason University

Corporations:
- Microsoft
- Boeing
- Coca Cola
- Disney
- Intel Corporation

Figure 3. TMUs in the public and private sectors

Below are more detailed examples of TMUs currently operating within the public sector.

Department of Defense: NCIS

While there are many TMUs functioning in public and private sectors, the Task Force found only one example of an operational TMU within the DoD – the Naval Criminal Investigative Service (NCIS) TMU. The NCIS TMU was established in 1996 as a result of a rise in workplace violence, stalking, and threatening communications. The NCIS TMU is a 24-hour proactive cooperation capability used to provide immediate analysis and assessment of concerning/threatening behaviors. The TMU assists the field and commands with complex and potentially dangerous investigations, provides risk assessments which places the communication and/or threatening behavior on a continuum of potential violence, and provides recommendations regarding investigative strategies and security-related solutions.

The NCIS TMU consists of three full-time NCIS Special Agents, two part time NCIS Analysts, and one NCIS Staff Psychologist, all located in the NCIS Headquarters (NCISHQ). Additionally, there are 70 trained NCIS Special Agents and Investigators who work TMU issues as a collateral duty in the field. On an ad hoc basis, other professionals such as legal, Family Advocacy Program (FAP), medical/mental health, Chaplains, and HR (Human Resources) provide insight and assistance with the assessment.

The NCIS TMU is consulted during investigations involving (but not limited to) stalking, workplace violence (WPV), wrongful destruction, crisis negotiations, school violence, threatening communications, terrorism, murder for hire, and serial crimes such as rape, child abuse, bomb threats, high-risk domestic violence, and kidnapping.

These investigations incorporate high-ranking Navy officials, command members, and dependents. The investigations occur in CONUS and OCONUS installations and locations. The types of investigations include criminal, counter-intelligence, as well as counter-terrorism matters. To date, violence was averted in each case in which the TMU was consulted. Referrals to the TMU can be made directly to NCIS, or indirectly via Text Tip, hotline, email, letter, third party, or any other means of communication.

Department of Justice: FBI

The Federal Bureau of Investigation (FBI) has adopted threat assessment principles through its Behavioral Analysis Unit (BAU). The BAU is a component of the National Center for the Analysis of Violent Crime (NCAVC), Critical Incident Response Group. The Behavioral Threat Assessment Center (BTAC) is housed within the BAU-1's Counterterrorism and Threat Assessment Unit. The BTAC consists of two FBI Supervisory Special Agents, two FBI Crime Analysts, one U.S. Capitol Police Task Force Agent, and one ad hoc ATF Task Force Agent. The BTAC also routinely utilizes a contracted licensed psychiatrist to support assessments. The BTAC is supported by the hundreds of FBI agents who volunteer at their respective FBI field offices for the collateral assignment as an NCAVC Coordinator.

The BTAC's mission is to provide operational threat assessment and threat management support to the many federal, state, and local agencies who must respond to each threatening communication or report of disturbing behavior. With prevention of violence as the primary focus, the BTAC offers services in matters involving targeted violence, lone offenders, active shooters, campus attackers, threats against public officials and Members of Congress, public figure stalking, and the analysis of communicated threats. BTAC personnel routinely provide threat identification, assessment, and management strategies in support of complex domestic and international investigations. The BTAC works cooperatively with other threat assessment and law enforcement safety professionals to develop short-term mitigation and long-term threat management strategies to reduce the likelihood of a violent attack.

United States Capitol Police

The Threat Assessment Section (TAS) of the U.S. Capitol Police was founded in 1986 as a dedicated unit to investigate threats against Members of Congress. The TAS is responsible for investigating threats against Members of Congress, their families, staff, and other statutory protectees. In addition, the TAS actively participates in the threat management of problematic individuals in the effort to minimize any potential risk of violence against Members of Congress. The TAS currently has 13 assigned Agents. In 2011, the TAS conducted approximately 4000 investigations involving threats and inappropriate contact with Congressional Offices.

University of Nebraska-Lincoln

Targeted violence on educational campuses has been on the rise over the last several years leading many academic institutions to establish TMUs. Since 2001, the University of Nebraska-Lincoln (UNL) has operated a Threat Assessment Team (TAT). The TAT was created and operates by organizing existing resources. The team avoids supplanting normal university functions by focusing upon the assessment and management of safety and risk issues.

UNL has successfully implemented a TAT that has addressed dozens of situations (e.g., threats from internal and external sources to the campus, human resource concerns, student/staff welfare, stalking). It consists of officers specially trained in threat assessment, as well as a consulting psychologist. Other campus personnel (such as those in human resources, mental health, and student services) participate on an as-needed basis. The university's police department has primary responsibility for the security of the campus and properties, and the investigation of criminal incidents occurring on university grounds. University stakeholders can make a referral via any university official or directly (e.g., in person, via text, phone, email, or anonymously via web site) for a threat assessment when encountering a concerning behavior.

In addition to training sessions to encourage prevention and early reporting, TAT members also reach out to human resources and student affairs staff with guidelines and criteria for use in screening for problematic student or employee issues that may raise concerns or warrant referrals. The TAT also monitors campus and local police contacts for incidents (e.g., domestic violence, protection orders, and stalking allegations) that may warrant further assessment or monitoring of potential threats to the campus setting. Additionally, TAT members coordinate interventions with other university services, as well as monitor situations as warranted, to ensure that there is no flare-up of a posed threat. As a key focus, the TAT has educated and collaborated with a wide range of university stakeholder groups.

Los Angeles Police Department

The Los Angeles Police Department (LAPD), serving a city of 3.8 million, formed its TMU in 1990 to investigate and manage the long-term threatening behavior often associated with obsessed individuals. Due to the sensitive nature of these investigations, the TMU is often tasked with performing discrete threat utilization by utilizing non-traditional methods of intervention in lieu of arrest and prosecution. As a result, relationships with the mental health community have been expanded and the use of civil protective orders has gained widespread acceptance as an intervention tool.

Presently, the TMU is tasked with the investigation of aggravated criminal, and at times non-criminal, cases of stalking and criminal threats on a city-wide basis. The LAPD's TMU currently has seven assigned Detectives with city-wide investigative responsibilities, and has averaged between 200-240 complex or aggravated stalking/threat related cases per year since its inception.

3.4.3   The Importance of TMUs

Some institutions that have suffered through attacks of targeted violence suggested that enhanced communication between stakeholders and coordinated interventions could have been instrumental in identifying and perhaps even thwarting the violent plan. For instance, in the aftermath of the attack at Virginia Tech, a panel convened by then Governor Tim Kaine reviewed the University's actions prior to and during the attack. One of the key findings noted by the panel was:

> *"During Cho's junior year at Virginia Tech, numerous incidents occurred that were clear warnings of mental instability. Although various individuals and departments within the university knew about each of these incidents, the university did not intervene effectively. No one knew all the information and no one connected all the dots.*[10]

The panel subsequently recommended that:

> **"Virginia Tech and other institutions of higher learning should have a threat assessment team that includes representatives from law enforcement, human resources, student and academic affairs, legal counsel, and mental health functions.** *The team should be empowered to take actions such as additional investigation, gathering background information, identification of additional dangerous warning signs, establishing a threat potential risk level (1 to 10) for a case, preparing a case for*

---

[10] "Mass Shootings at Virginia Tech, April 16, 2007," *Report of the Virginia Tech Review Panel Presented to Timothy M. Kaine, Governor Commonwealth of Virginia,* (August 2007): 1.

hearings (for instance, commitment hearings), and disseminating warning information."[11]

Further, the Ft. Hood review panel recognized the significance of such organizations and recommended the Department pursue incorporating best practices and policies of existing TMUs, noting specifically the NCIS TMU. The panel issued the following recommendation in the Final Review Report (3.2):

> *"Develop policy and procedures to integrate the currently disparate efforts to defend DoD resources and people against internal threats.*
>
> *Commission a multidisciplinary group to examine and evaluate existing threat assessment programs; examine other branches of government for successful programs and best practices to establish standards, training, reporting requirements, and procedures for assessing predictive indicators relating to pending violence.*
>
> *Provide commanders with a multidisciplinary capability, based on best practices such as the Navy's Threat Management Unit, the Postal Service's "Going Postal Program," and Stanford University's workplace violence program, focused on predicting and preventing insider attacks."[12]*

Perhaps one of the most important features of a cohesive and operational TMU is the information sharing practices between stakeholders performing protection type missions. As highlighted in the Fort Hood Report:

> *"Detecting and defeating an internal threat requires close personal observation and interaction rather than the construction of physical security barriers…There is no DoD-wide protocol to notify commanders of potential threats that may exist in their command…The effort to identify threats may be enhanced by exploiting any common indicators and integrating the disparate programs designed to defend against these threats."[13]*

Additionally, the update to DoD Instruction (DODI) 6495.02 – Sexual Assault Prevention and Response Program, once approved and published, will require each Service to establish a multidisciplinary Case Management Group (CMG), a structure which is similar to the TMU model. Although DoDI 6495.02 focuses on adult sexual assault vice work place violence, the instruction requires behavioral assessments of criminal acts similar to Threat Management practices. Assessments of behaviors of concern can be done by the same trained group of professionals. In the current environment of diminishing resources, organizations are encouraged to evaluate operations and create efficiencies to meet the growing demand for leaner, more efficient operations. It cannot be overlooked that adult sexual assault and work place violence possess similarities especially in regards to behaviors of concern. Many of the issues contained in DoDI 6495.02 relate to stalking, suicide, threats, and other criminal acts

---

[11] Ibid., 19.

[12] Ibid., 28

[13] "Protecting the Force: Lessons from Fort Hood," *Report of the DoD Independent Review,* (January 2010): 26.

similar to the same crimes investigated by TMUs. Additional issues of relevance include performing safety assessments and risk assessments, regular attendance and participation in a monthly deliberative case evaluation panel, and trained and certified representatives from various installation level organizations.

Since the 2007 shootings at Virginia Tech, insurance companies have received negligence claims against educational institutions arising from incidents of targeted violence on campus. In some of these cases, the institution had no threat assessment team. The Task Force received input from one academic insurance representative supporting the need for threat assessment team to avert increasing one's liability during work place violence incidents. For example, plaintiffs' lawyers argue that failing to establish a threat assessment team violates a standard of care. When states, such as Virginia and Illinois, pass laws (see Appendix 9) requiring colleges to create these teams and several public and private entities reviewing campus security also recommend them, plaintiffs allege that the absence of such a team directly correlates to the institutions low regard for work place violence. Additionally, plaintiffs and their lawyers allege that if an employee of an institution has knowledge about an individual's troubling behavior that knowledge extends to the institution and triggers an institutional duty to respond reasonably - even if the employee never tells anyone else on campus about the behavior. Moreover, this claim of a duty to respond is often supported by the institution's own policies, which may require employees to report or take certain actions in response to disturbing employee or student behaviors. When there is no threat assessment team to receive these reports and coordinate the institution's timely response, plaintiffs typically argue this shows negligence - an argument that is particularly compelling in the aftermath of a tragedy.

The various TMUs that are in operation address a wide spectrum of concerning and threatening behaviors. Although it is impossible to quantify the number of violent incidents averted due to TMU intervention, there can be no doubt that the TMU's proactive practices and risk management strategies have saved lives, mitigated risk, and decreased an organization's liability.

3.5   TMU Operations

In each case and more generally, there are basic tenets that are important to successful operation of the TMU. They must be perceived as trustworthy and able to protect the privacy of those reporting a concerning behavior. They must also be seen as fair, helping to alleviate concerns over stigma, false-positives, and negative career impacts that may result from arbitrary or unfair analysis. Finally, threat management cannot work without trained professionals, community awareness, and effective communications strategies.

3.5.1   TMU Mission and Goals

The mission of the TMU is to prevent targeted violence by developing calculated responses to troubling behaviors.[14] The goal of the TMUs is to identify and assess individuals or groups who demonstrate behaviors of concern, threats of violence, or acts of aggression towards others

---

[14] Radicalization can be a motivating factor in targeted violence. TMUs can address this successfully by focusing on responses to *behaviors*, rather than targeting specific demographics, religious adherents, or political views.

and the workplace. The TMU may evaluate threats or indicators of self-harm in certain circumstances where the potential for harm to others concurrently exists. The TMU will conduct a systematic elimination of nonthreatening situations to effectively guide the use of resources and to contribute to the reduction of inappropriate behavior and facilitate conflict resolution. The TMU should be empowered to offer threat mitigation strategies and risk abatement plans that serve the best interests of stakeholders, to include the DoD, potential victims, and possible perpetrators. These strategies will be consistent with DoD protocols and policies. The TMU will promote dignity and respect as opposed to an intrusive, arbitrary or heavy-handed approach while providing a solid assessment of the potential risk for violence. These assessments will help the DoD make informed decisions about the safety of its installations, personnel, and products.

3.5.2   TMU Structure

The recommended structure of a TMU consists of three to four headquarters-level agents with field-level TMU duties assigned as collateral duty. The headquarters-level agents are expected to operate as full-time members of the TMU and are expected to develop subject matter expertise in the area of threat assessment. The TMU is a cross-functional, multidisciplinary team approach to assist in assessing threatening situations and developing risk abatement plans that minimize the potential risk for violence. This model does not necessitate assigning legions of detailees across every facet of an organization. Just the opposite, an effective capability can be achieved with a structure as described above, working in tandem with a small number of trained, multi-disciplinary specialists (intelligence analysts, psychologists, human resource professionals, medical care providers, social workers/family advocates, chaplains, and lawyers) who contribute to the TMU as collateral duty. This model is not costly to implement – and provides value far in excess of its direct cost to the host organization.

Appropriately trained threat assessment professionals take into consideration multiple behavioral and risk factors prior to making an assessment. An informed assessment must involve the consideration of contextual, mitigation, risk, and resilience factors; and potential stressors. The TMU must possess access to sufficient, credible, first-hand collateral data sources; must be able to assess the impact of gathering information; use the investigative/threat assessment process; and avoid over-reliance on single factors (factors considered must be scientifically relevant or those considered within the field based upon empirical and published literature). The trained threat assessor, when conceptualizing risk level, must recognize professional limitations pertinent to the threat assessment and seek out relevant consultation or expertise when necessary. The assessor must qualify the assessment when necessary and must be aware of the complex contextual, legal, ethical, and regulatory issues that impact the violence risk assessment process. Certain triage questions should be asked. Those questions include, but are not limited to:

- Has there been any mention of suicidal thoughts, plans, or attempts?
- Has there been any mention of thoughts or plans of violence?
- Have there been any behaviors that cause concern for violence or the person's well-being?

- Does the person have access or are they trying to gain access to a weapon (contextually inappropriate)?
- Are there behaviors that are significantly disruptive to the workplace environment?

Having collected all of the relevant information pertaining to the person or communication of concern, the TMU will then provide an assessment of the potential risk of violence, investigative suggestions, and threat management strategies to reduce the potential for a violent attack. The TMU documents all findings, recommendations, and suggested strategies. While short-term strategies may resolve a situation, often times a long-term case management approach is necessary as problematic behaviors change, evolve, or reorient toward a new target. As updated information is developed, the threat assessment team needs the flexibility and agility to respond and react to the changing threatscape. Figure 4 illustrates the TMU headquarters and field reporting structure.

The TMU can act as a resource and offer support, including information and recommendations. The TMU will act in the best interests of the DoD members and the DoD community and will follow up on any incident to ensure that the threat is mitigated.

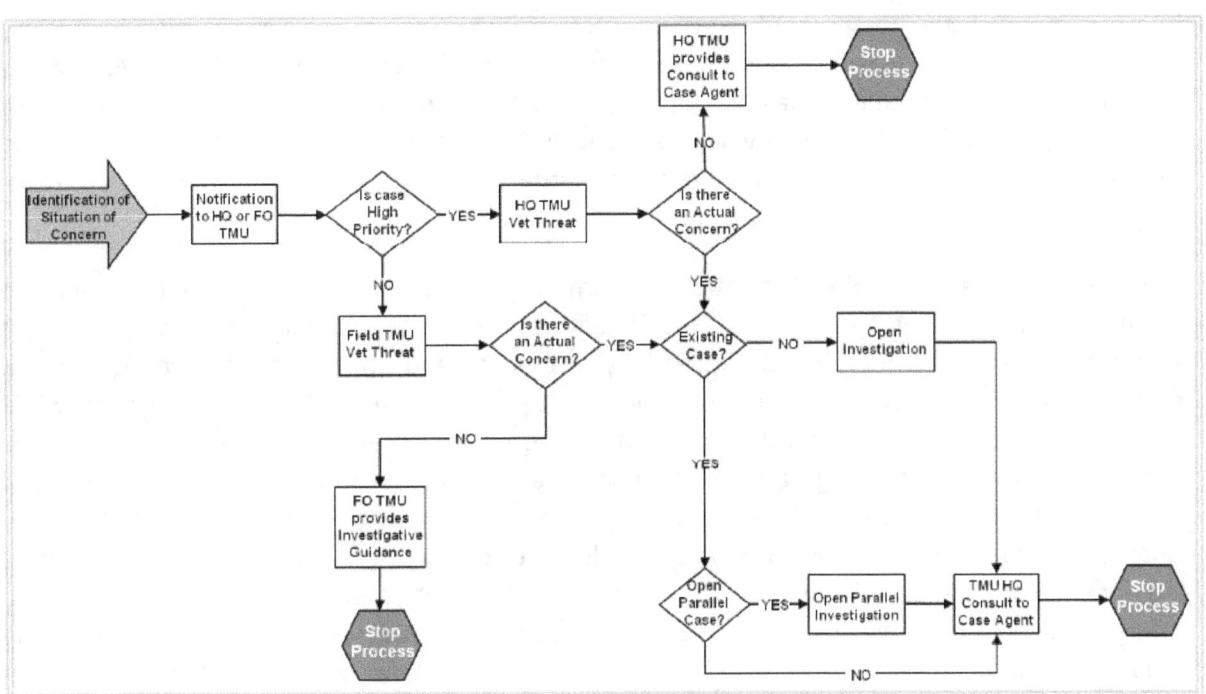

Figure 4. Headquarters and Field TMU Reporting Schematic (NCIS)

3.5.3   TMU Training

The TMU can achieve its goals by developing and maintaining subject matter experts/expertise in threat assessment disciplines through extended professional development, to include allowing for extended tours of duty in TMUs in order to foster the necessary depth of knowledge required to assess and mitigate threats. At a minimum, core members of the TMU need to receive annual training to maintain expertise through exposure to evolving threat assessment methodologies and strategies. Ad-hoc TMU members should also be considered for less intensive but equally informative and relevant training. Other stakeholders in the community should also receive training that is focused on delivery of recognition strategies and reporting mechanisms.

Awareness training for bystanders and other potential reporters of concerning behavior can involve various multi-modal communications channels. This facilitates wide-aperture reports of concerning behaviors via American Forces Network (AFN), base security marquees, annual training, distance learning/virtual training, Text Tip, and/or routine briefings.

3.5.4 Successful Threat Management Case Examples/Thwarted Attacks

1) FBI Behavioral Analysis Unit/Behavioral Threat Assessment Center

A college sophomore at a major university began displaying increasing bizarre and hostile behaviors to classmates and professors. His roommates reported that the male student had demonstrated an increasing interest in firearms acquisition and practice. The student also became increasingly hostile to his roommates, drawing target circles on pictures of his cohabitants. With increasing signs of deterioration and violent ideation, there were many indicators of problematic behavior but no actions or behaviors to sustain an arrest or involuntary mental health care evaluation. The BAU/BTAC worked with campus, local, and federal authorities, as well as mental health care professionals, to assess the student's potential risk of escalation from ideation to violence.

After examining all available information concerning the student's functioning and history, the team determined that the student's rapid deterioration and concurrent escalation in his interest in firearms were signs of potentially significant and imminent violence. The threat assessment team swiftly crafted a mitigation plan to address the problematic behaviors while recognizing that neither detention nor arrest were available options. The focus of the mitigation plan was the forging of a bond between the investigators and the student. The student appeared to lack any meaningful rapport with a responsible adult, and the team determined that such a connection would facilitate disclosures related to escalation, plans of violence, and possible willingness to voluntarily submit to mental health care treatment. Informed and trained investigators conducted a thorough threat assessment interview of the student, focusing on issues related to his social functioning, struggles at school, and the lack of any available support system to help him cope with contextual stressors. That resulted in the student's decision to voluntarily submit to in-patient mental health treatment. Subsequent to the interview, a loaded handgun was located under the student's car seat. The mental health care practitioner's evaluation characterized the student as a "ticking time bomb" and that an attack had been a question of "when, not if." The student received treatment and subsequently dropped out of college. He has not engaged in any act of targeted violence against the campus or the roommates.

2) Los Angeles Police Department's Threat Management Unit

In April 2008 a 33 year city employee assigned to the Department of Water and Power (DWP), attended a scheduled doctor appointment for an ongoing medical condition. During routine questioning by the staff nurse, the employee advised that he was depressed and suicidal due to continuous hazing by co-workers. The employee provided the nurse with a handwritten list of 16 co-workers that he wanted to torture and kill. The employee had envisioned that one day he would drive to work in a large truck, block the exit, and then "massacre" everyone on his hit list. Based on the threats, the medical staff notified DWP security, who in-turn notified the TMU.

Once involved, TMU detectives intervened and worked with the medical staff to secure an involuntary mental evaluation for the employee. TMU members then coordinated with the City Attorney's office to obtain restraining orders on behalf of the 16 targeted city employees. Upon his discharge from the psychiatric facility, the employee was served with the restraining orders and was interviewed by TMU detectives at his home. The employee was prescribed anti-depressant medication and participated in an out-patient treatment program. The employee remains under the restrictions of the restraining orders and periodic welfare checks by TMU personnel confirmed that he is complying with his out-patient treatment.

3) Naval Criminal Investigative Service's Threat Management Unit

A subject, his wife, and his girlfriend all worked for the same Navy command. All were civilian engineers with high level security clearances. During an argument, the subject told his wife he was going to leave her for his girlfriend and would sell "crypto" to a foreign government. The subject's wife notified NCIS that the subject was quick to use physical violence in order to exert control over situations.

The investigation subsequently revealed that the subject had historically displayed poor judgment on classified issues as well as behavioral concerns. The subject's outbursts and violent tendencies led supervisors to avoid disciplinary action or document problematic behaviors due to fear of reprisal. Co-workers and supervisors also reported being so intimidated by the subject that they would avoid giving him work for fear he would lose his temper.

The subject had also been violent outside of the workplace, while on Temporary Assigned Duty (TAD) orders as well as with a prior employer, prompting the local police to respond on numerous occasions. The subject had a history of inappropriate behavior that had not been reported to command.

The subject was eventually terminated due to loss of his clearance and his behavior toward members of the command. For approximately two years after his termination, he continued to harass the command members, including his ex-wife. The subject's history of violence and intimidation was so profound that the command members were still in fear of the subject even though he was no longer an employee. Every time the subject resurfaced, the command contacted the NCIS TMU. The harassment was documented by the TMU in order to identify and measure problematic behaviors. Specific threat management measures were developed and implemented by the TMU to deter the subject from accessing command members. The subject was eventually arrested by local police officials for assaulting his girlfriend. He eventually moved to another state and found other employment.

3.6   Recommendations

The Secretary of Defense direct a Department-wide requirement for the Military Departments and DoD Agencies to establish a multidisciplinary TMU that identifies, assesses, and responds/manages threats of targeted violence.

- Designate an Executive Agent (EA) responsible for overseeing and managing the Department's TMUs. The EA would be responsible for management, oversight, identifying resources and training requirements, and serve as DoD's central point for threat management – with OSD policy oversight.

- Charter the Executive Agent to conduct operationally relevant research on the nature and extent of targeted violence affecting the DoD community in order to inform the operation of TMUs.

The designated Executive Agent should establish effective information sharing and communications among DoD TMUs and with appropriate non-DoD organizations:

- Establish an information sharing system that would facilitate the review and assessment of communications or behaviors of concern for immediate use by the TMUs and for analytic purposes.

- Develop and implement a communication strategy to establish a higher level of awareness regarding the risk of targeted violence throughout DoD. This should include methods of messaging to the DoD community and establishing multimodal response channels to optimize the capture of critical threat reports.

- Efforts dealing with this violent behavior should take advantage of the significant overlap and be integrated as appropriate with related efforts including suicide prevention, impulsive violence, sexual harassment, early warning signs of Post-Traumatic Stress Disorder (PTSD), and coping with medical or financial stress, particularly with respect to the professional resources involved and associated training programs.

4.0 Limitations on Sharing Information

Information was available in many of the cases where service members engaged in acts of targeted violence prior to the violent act that either (1) suggested the individual contemplated harming himself or others, (2) was in need of help due to stressful life circumstances, (3) was otherwise isolated from his colleagues, depressed, or engaged in questionable associations or activities, or (4) combinations of the foregoing. Relevant information might have been known to co-workers, family members or neighbors; or even supervisors and commanders. In some cases relevant information was known to medical or law enforcement personnel. In many instances the information was ignored, suppressed, or otherwise failed to result in diversion, intervention, or effective help being provided to the individual prior to the violent act. Strands of information which in isolation may be of dubious relevancy when shared, compiled, and analyzed may present a compelling case for intervention. Likewise specific information that indicates an imminent violent act needs to be expedited to authorities in a position to prevent the act. The Task Force encountered two broad categories of information sharing limitations: Privacy/Religious Accommodation and Organizational.

Information Sharing Limitations—Privacy and Religious Accommodation Issues

Improved sharing of information while potentially useful as a tool in detecting and preventing potential targeted violence also presents the risk of intrusive and offensive encroachment on personal privacy. In our society personal privacy is generally a cherished cultural value. It should be recognized that the tension between protection of personal privacy and other important public policy objectives has broad implications. This includes statutory law and even has a Constitutional dimension.

In 1965 the Supreme Court found a "right of privacy" in the shadowy "penumbra of the Constitution" but dissenting Justices at that time and many critics since argued such a right is not found in any specific provision or provisions of the Constitution and simply does not exist. However, the constitutional "right of privacy" has been applied by the Court with profound effects. While controversial, there seems to be little doubt that many Americans associate themselves with the idea that the Constitution guarantees a "right of privacy" in some sense. This cautions that intrusions of personal privacy should occur only when necessary and be done with circumspection. However, the Court has also noted that the demands of the military may limit or modify certain Constitutional rights for service members. The same limitations do not necessarily apply to other, non-military personnel that may have business on military installations though the needs of the military may have impacts on their rights as well.

4.1   Privacy Act and HIPAA Privacy Rule

In discussing information sharing in the context of forecasting or preventing violent behavior two statutes are particularly pertinent. These statutes have different objectives and different procedures but they also overlap to a degree in that certain "agency records" and "systems of records" regulated by the Privacy Act contain "personal health information" and are also subject to the Privacy Rule of HIPAA.

The Privacy Act of 1974 regulates the way certain types of information may be acquired and used by the Federal Government and provides certain rights to individuals whose information is acquired by the government. While the pertinent provisions of the Privacy Act will be outlined below it is worth stating up front some of the things the Privacy Act does not regulate. The Privacy Act does not regulate information that is shared through routine conversation and inter-personal interaction not involving "agency records." It does not regulate private records such as notes a commander might make with respect to his personnel when such notes are used as an adjunct to the commander's memory and are never placed in an agency system of records. DoD and its components have issued various regulations and guidance implementing the Privacy Act.

Appendix 11 contains a summary of pertinent provisions of the Privacy Act, guidance on certain DoD-specific applications of the Act, and the text of pertinent DoD "blanket routine uses." A 240-page overview of the Act can be found at http://www.justice.gov/opcl/1974privacyact.pdf.

Enacted in 1996 the Health Insurance Portability and Accountability Act was amended in 2003 to add provisions relating to "protected health information" which apply to the Federal Government as well as to private sector organizations. Protected health information includes certain information transmitted verbally as well as written records. The Department of Health and Human Services is charged with overseeing regulations implementing the Act. The DoD has issued guidance regarding provisions of the HIPAA Privacy Rule that specifically apply to the military.

Appendix 12 presents an outline of the HIPAA Privacy Rule, a summary of 45 CFR 164.512(k), and DoD 6025.18-R, the military specific application of the Rule.

4.2   Privacy Issues: Perceptions and Faulty Implementation

The Task Force received various presentations with serious differences of opinion regarding whether the Privacy Act and the HIPAA Privacy Rule, particularly the latter, inhibited the sharing of information within DoD and among DoD and other agencies in ways that were detrimental to identifying individuals inclined to commit acts of targeted violence.

First, it is clear that the two statutes create an administrative burden and do, without doubt, inhibit the flow of information that could occur without them. It is much less clear that when thoughtfully and accurately implemented they constitute a critical barrier to the flow of essential information in most relevant instances or that they are weighted in favor of privacy interests in a way that is fundamentally inconsistent with other important public policy issues including identifying factors indicative of potential targeted violence.

The divergent views on this subject presented to the Task Force clearly indicate that privacy rules are not applied consistently throughout the Department and in some cases they constitute a barrier to the effective flow of information. A serious review of the implementation of privacy rules and their potential for adverse impacts should be undertaken. The DoD can take a number of steps to mitigate adverse impacts including enhanced education, and modification of directives and Privacy Act record systems notices. If such steps are insufficient legislative proposals to correct deficiencies needing legislative modification should be undertaken.

4.3   Religious Practice

In today's diverse and multi-cultural America we have come a long way from religious attitudes present at the founding of the Republic. As originally enacted the Constitution was recorded as having been signed in the "year of our Lord." Justice Joseph Story writing in his acclaimed Commentaries on the Constitution (1833) states that the framers and drafters of the First Amendment probably agreed that promotion of Christianity was good. The probable primary intent of the drafters of the First Amendment of the Constitution was not to countenance religions such as Islam ("Mahometanism") but was to exclude rivalries among Christian sects and preclude the creation of a national ecclesiastical establishment, any such establishment being exclusively in the province of the States. Justice Story goes on to say that the free exercise clause means that a person's religious belief, presumably though not expressly stated by Justice Story including Islam, is not a matter for inquiry at the federal level.

One apparent confirmation of Justice Story's view that the First Amendment was meant to avoid rivalry among Christian sects is the long history and continuation of the military chaplaincy. However, even that has been modified by the inclusion of non-Christian religions in that institution. Moreover, the caveat that Constitutional rights of service members may be more restricted than for the general public applies in this area as well. Current DoD policy recognizes this.

Current DoD policy regarding religious accommodation is found in DoD Instruction (DODI) 1300.17 titled "Accommodation of Religious Practices Within the Military Services". The general policy is that requests for accommodation of religious practices should be approved as long as they do not adversely impact on military readiness, unit cohesion, standards, or discipline, or, otherwise interfere with the service member's duties. Guidance developed under civil sector Civil Rights laws is helpful in understanding this issue. Service members should not be treated more or less favorably based on their religion. They cannot be required to participate or refrain from participating in a religious activity as part of their duties. Reasonable accommodation of practices based on sincerely held religious belief should be accommodated subject to the conditions outlined in DoDI 1300.17. Finally, a commander must take steps to halt religious harassment of members of his command.

One contentious area is that of proselytizing. Although service members have the right to engage in religious conduct consistent with DoDI 1300.17, proselytizing by one service member may be viewed as religious harassment by another who is the object of the proselytizing. Dealing with this issue requires balancing of divergent interests. Consideration should be given to the pervasiveness of the proselytizing, whether other service members believe they are being harassed, and any possible impact on duty performance, for example.

The fact that the free exercise of religion is a Constitutional right and that DoD policy favors accommodation of religious practices in no way protects activities that may be evidence of an intent to commit violent acts, otherwise harm others, or disrupt the military mission. Such activities even though clothed in religious terminology or undertaken in a religious context are not immunized from scrutiny and appropriate action. Personnel should feel free to convey pertinent information to appropriate authorities when their suspicions are aroused even if such reporting involves someone's religious statements or activities.

The Task Force reviewed case studies which indicated radical religious doctrines have played an important role in several high profile cases of targeted violence both within and outside the military. Violent actors were sometimes radicalized by association with other religious radicals and sometimes "self-radicalized." While a number of cases involved radical Islam, there were examples involving Christianity, and the potential exists for radicalization to occur in the context of other religions as well.

Targeted violence often involves a variety of factors motivating the perpetrator. Covering over or ignoring radical religious belief as a potential factor will greatly handicap efforts to discover and divert individuals who are on a trajectory toward engaging in targeted violence. Therefore, it will be necessary for personnel engaged in understanding and preventing targeted violence to be able to discern amongst the various means of professing religious faith that which expressly promotes violence or is radical in nature.

4.4   Information Sharing Limitations--Organizational

During the course of its work, the Task Force encountered some information sharing limitations originating from organizational construct and practices. Although organizational boundaries are not inherently restrictive, the Task Force encountered several instances in which organizational boundaries and practices inhibited the flow of information necessary to prevent targeted violence incidents.

4.5   Personnel Records Information Sharing

Commanders and supervisors are held responsible for the behavior of their personnel. However, some of the very tools required to keep commanders and supervisors informed often restrict their access. The DoD Independent Review Related to Fort Hood found the only information remaining with an individual throughout his or her career was either performance related or medical. Neither of these categories of files lends themselves to review by a commander or supervisor in the assessment of an individual's behavior.

Following the final Fort Hood review, the Secretary of Defense directed the Chairman, Joint Chiefs of Staff and the Service Chiefs of the Military Departments to determine procedures for appropriate documentation of behaviors detrimental to good order and discipline, particularly those that could be associated with violence, prohibited activities, and potential harm to self and others. A Joint Staff sponsored working group was formed to address this issue.

The Chairman's response to the Secretary, dated 21 March 2011, summarized the working group's findings that current personnel related programs, processes and procedures already document violent conduct and further actions pursuing amendment of official personnel files is not required. While the PVB TF supports this finding of adequate documentation, documentation without adequate access to the information contained in the documentation does not solve the problem identified by the Secretary. The TF felt more needs to be done to give commanders more visibility into information concerning individuals transferring from a losing location. At present, each new assignment for an individual represents a "clean slate" whereby concerning behaviors is not documented across assignments, patterns get lost, and prevention becomes significantly more challenging.

Subsequently, the Joint Staff-sponsored working group identified two additional gaps it felt warranted further study by the DSB's PVB Task Force:

(1) Lack of reporting/visibility for commanders/supervisors on Service members' conduct;

(2) Lack of key definitions and business rules for dealing with violent behaviors.

The PVB TF agreed that these gaps exist. Commanders/supervisors still do not have sufficient visibility into the personnel records of those transferring into their command/organizations, and have no organized (or "business rules") way to get help in resolving concerning behaviors issues. The Task Force believes that implementing a threat management approach systematically in the Department, as it recommends, along with the information sharing reforms it also recommends, will address both of these gaps.

In addition to the organizational construct that inhibits information flow between gaining and losing commands discussed above the Task Force noted one significantly different organizational construct involving the Department of the Army. With the exception of the Department of the Army, the other Military Departments currently operate a centralized, combined intelligence, counter intelligence and law enforcement threat information sharing capability. The Task Force felt that the separation of these key entities in any organization perpetuates failure and significantly limits an organization's ability to accurately access the nature of any type of threat. The current relationship between the U.S. Army Intelligence and Security Command (INSCOM), the U.S. Army Criminal Investigation Command (CID), and law enforcement should be revaluated with the goal of operating in a more integrated manner without inserting organizational boundaries as potential barriers to the rapid flow of relevant information.

4.6 National Threat Information Sharing

In the aftermath of the tragic shooting of U.S. military personnel at Fort Hood in November 2009, the President of the United States convened a meeting of his key officials, the heads of intelligence and security agencies and the DoD to assess what went wrong. The end analysis, an age old problem that continues to plague our Nation today...the reluctance to share time-critical and sometimes sensitive information to the right people, both interdepartmentally and with external partners.

The DoD Independent Review Related to Fort Hood concluded that gaps do in fact exists in providing information to the right people but to further complicate relationships, Services, DoD components and our various partner agencies operate internally within stove pipes relative to the types of information collected and managed...intelligence; counterintelligence; terrorism/counterterrorism; law enforcement, and force protection. The review recommended "the Department could and should do more. The time has passed when bureaucratic concerns by specific entities over protecting "their" information can be allowed to prevent relevant threat information and indicators from reaching those who need it-commanders."[15]

The Follow-on Review found that not all information sharing relationships will be improved through formal agreements. At the local and international level, current information sharing policies and procedures are adequate. Attempts to formalize these information sharing relationships will be counterproductive, since this approach would convey a lack of trust and reduce partners' incentives to cooperate by increasing their administrative and legal burdens. Therefore, the Follow-On Review found that the Department could benefit from formal agreements for a limited set of force protection threat information sharing relationships.[16]

4.7   Information Sharing Today

Over the course of 10 months, the TF received briefings from Departmental organizations including INSCOM, Army G-2X, Army G34 Protection, the Office of the Under Secretary of Defense (Intelligence), and the FBI. Information sharing, internal and external to the Department entailed a myriad of information types warranting evaluation, including Intelligence, Counter-terrorism and Law Enforcement. The TF focused its efforts primarily on sharing of Force Protection Threat Information.

There are many complexities surrounding the types of information to be shared, whom the recipients should be, and how frequently information should be shared. Throughout the TF's research, a reoccurring theme emerged: threat information sharing, internal and external to DoD, still has gaps. In addition to the briefings the Task Force received, the Co-Chairs independently sought perspectives from additional agencies on how successful attempts have been to share information outside the Department. The Co-Chairs met with personnel from the Office of the Assistant Secretary of Defense for Homeland Defense and Americas' Security Affairs (OASD(HD&ASA)), the National Joint Terrorism Task Force (NJTTF), and the Defense Counterintelligence and Human Intelligence Center (DCHC). Unanimously, all three agencies provided positive feedback on improvements since the tragic shootings at Fort Hood. Unfortunately, without reservation, all three agreed there are still gaps but with future

---

[15] Report of the DoD Independent Review, January 2010.

[16] Final Recommendations of the Ft. Hood Follow-On Review, August 18, 2010.

enhancements to existing programs, policies and relationships, more improvements should be recognized.

The Department stood up a Force Protection Senior Steering Group to oversee DoD's implementation of the Fort Hood final review. To better manage the volume of effort envisioned in addressing all the recommendations, five working groups were designated, one of which addresses Threat Information Sharing.

Additionally, the Department initiated several initiatives to address the lingering information sharing gaps. In the months following Fort Hood, two internal documents underwent review and revision, DoDI 5240.22 (Counterintelligence Support to Force Protection) and DoDI 2000.12, (DoD Antiterrorism (AT) Program). Both of these instructions address information shortfalls identified in the Ft. Hood Report.

The National Joint Terrorism Task Force, congressionally funded and tasked with the Nation's Counterterrorism mission, promotes direct sharing between the Department and the FBI. Each JTTF office differs in size and mission and to some degree comprises representatives from the Department of Defense. At the time of this report, 57% of the JTTFs has DoD representation. The determination to provide DoD representation at a particular JTTF involved analysis of historical data, evaluation of the impact of new processes and capabilities (e.g. eGuardian), and input from several DoD organizations (e.g. Joint Staff, Defense Intelligence Agency, Military Departments, OSD). DoD representation at specific JTTFs will be addressed every three years and the process includes an ability to immediately assign a DoD representative to any of the remaining 43% of the JTTFs without current DoD representation. This relationship provides the Department with dedicated advocates tasked with the responsibility of sharing real time threat information at the discretion of the Special Agent in Charge (SAC). This forum is viewed as a critical link to advancing information sharing between the Department and the FBI. The FBI invests heavily in training for JTTF members ensuring they receive relevant and timely training on handling and disseminating information. The FBI revised the training following the Ft Hood incident.

4.8   External Information Sharing

In the Department's efforts to improve information sharing outside DoD, specifically with the Federal Bureau of Investigation, the DoD and the FBI agreed to establish an overarching Memorandum of Understanding (MOU) titled "MOU Between FBI and DoD Governing the Sharing of Information and Operational Coordination" which would eliminate more than 100 information sharing agreements currently in existence. The MOU is intended to promote a more systemic, standardized, and controlled information sharing relationship between the two organizations and to clarify operational coordination procedures and investigative responsibilities.[17]

---

[17] *Memorandum of Understanding between the Federal Bureau of Investigation and the Department of Defense Governing Information Sharing, Operational Coordination, and Investigative Responsibilities*, August 2, 2011.

The MOU governs the FBI and DoD sharing of counterintelligence, counterterrorism, foreign intelligence, law enforcement, operational, and other information. The MOU applies to all components of the FBI and DoD. At the time this Task Force completed its information gathering effort; several annexes were in development to support the base agreement. Some annexes are already signed (e.g. The Counterterrorism Information Sharing, Counterintelligence Information Sharing, and the Terrorist Screening Information Sharing annexes) while completion of the other annexes is projected for December 2013. With the signing of these agreements along with updates to existing policies and programs, the foundation for improved sharing of threat information should help improve the gaps in the system today.

At present, threat information sharing represents a significant shift from historical norms. The Counterterrorism Information Sharing annex outlines that the FBI will notify the DoD National Military Command Center by the most expeditious means possible concerning time sensitive and/or immediate threats to the DoD. Although this process is in use, it is not without flaws. The information is not rendered in real time and there is no mechanism for ensuring the information gets to the right users in a timely manner. Further, there are instances where information flowed into the Department but didn't reach user levels. After information was passed from the FBI, there were no updates attesting to the FBI's investigative usefulness of the information. Conversely, neither the Military Departments nor Defense Agencies readily provided updates to the FBI on previously shared information.

The Counterterrorism Information Sharing annex also outlines the process the FBI uses to notify DoD of matters warranting additional investigative actions not considered to be time-sensitive and/or immediate threats to DoD. The FBI developed a redundant process to ensure the appropriate DoD investigative element responsible for international and/or domestic terrorism investigations is notified. Care should be taken that such processes aren't created to merely check the box on information sharing and actually meet the spirit with which information sharing is supposed to accomplish.

4.9   Recommendations

The General Counsel, collaboratively with other elements of the Department, develop clear and comprehensible guidance to provide better understanding to supervisors/ commanders of actual (as opposed to perceived) limitations on sharing of information:

- 1. Review the impact of privacy rules including those under the Privacy Act and HIPAA. If adverse impacts to the necessary flow of information are found, DoD should (1) take steps to mitigate those impacts, and, if found necessary (2) advance corrective legislative proposals.

- 2. DoD guidance (such as DoDI 1325.06, Handling Dissident and Protest Activity Among Military Members) should expressly state that religious speech or activities of a radical nature detrimental to DoD policy on conduct and behavior are not immunized from scrutiny merely by association with religious rhetoric or belief.

■ 3. Prepare concise, easily understood guidance on privacy and religious rules as they affect personnel actions and exchange of information on matters discussed in this report.

B. The Under Secretary of Defense for Intelligence and the Under Secretary of Defense for Policy, in coordination with the FBI, reassess DoD's current threat information sharing architecture both internal to the Department and externally with the goal of evaluating the migration of threat information down to the user level in a timely and thorough manner.

■ 1. As part of the assessment, DoD in collaboration with the FBI should develop a comprehensive, DoD-wide investigative database that would serve as a central repository of threat information. The database should be a collaborative endeavor ensuring all threat information is discoverable and accessible to trained threat management professionals experienced in sharing threat information with commanders and supervisors.

■ 2. Design a system of bench marks and metrics to be used to monitor and provide feedback from senior officials down to the user level on the effectiveness of information sharing practices and programs internal to the Department and with external partners.

C. The Department of the Army evaluate the organizational barriers that exist between INSCOM, CID and law enforcement and provide metrics to support current organizational constructs or develop new organizational constructs to improve the information flow.

5.0 Future Paths: Science and Technology

Behavioral markers may provide a measure of predictive capability regarding low occurrence, high consequence events like targeted violence. However, this predictive capability is far from reliable or certain. While such markers may be sensitive, they are of low specificity and thus carry the baggage of an unavoidable and costly false alarm rate, which limits feasibility of prediction-intervention strategies (see Appendix 13 – Prediction: Why It Won't Work for an illustration of why prediction is a difficult, if not impossible, approach). A more viable approach, analogous to examples found in other low occurrence and high consequence domains such as the management of nuclear weapons, is to start with the identification of individual, high impact influences or drivers – e.g., cognitive, emotional and motivational variables, as well as contextual determinants pertinent to targeted violence. Then one can establish risk management plans and mitigation efforts that can be applied broadly and may reduce the incidence of negative outcomes. This represents a focus on prevention/mitigation rather than prediction.

The challenge in preventing/mitigating violent behavior is further complicated by the number of contributing factors (social, genetic, neurological, psychological, physiological, etc.) and the variability from one person to the next. As illustrated in Figure 5, an individual's stress response curve displays a characteristic increase and plateau in performance under stress up to a tipping point (defined here as the point at which behavior is no longer predictable and is degraded with respect to contextually appropriate behavior), beyond which there is a decline. Such curves are highly specific to the individual and the particulars of the stress environment.

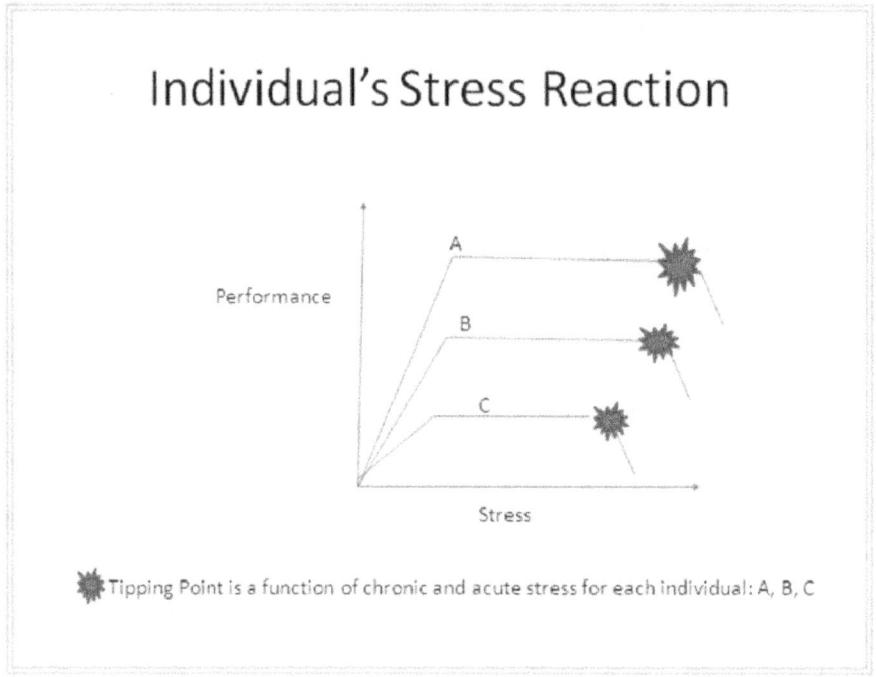

Figure 5. Notional Stress Response Curves

The decline can manifest itself in many ways — in the most extreme case, as targeted violence. However, there is evidence, supported by prior research and emerging science, that an individual's response to stress can be improved by increasing performance up to the tipping point and/or pushing out the tipping point on the stress-response curve; i.e., improving resiliency. Resiliency is defined here as the ability to recover from, or easily adjust to, misfortune or change, especially unanticipated change. The Task Force thus focused on improving resiliency by expanding the individual's ability to avoid a tipping point as a positive management approach to preventing/mitigating violent behavior.

Task Force believes a multi-faceted research program that builds on some promising starts in the Department of Defense is warranted. Specifically, the Task Force recommends:

- Collect and analyze behavioral science data in two domains:
    - o 1) case studies of violent behavior and;
    - o 2) merged personnel data bases as being initiated by the Army.

- Augment resilience training and assessment programs to measure key stress contributors (e.g., sleep deprivation, lack of personal connectedness) and effectiveness of resiliency training regimens.

- Initiate a biomarker-based measurement program to add "hard" data to the stress-resiliency database — first with physiological measures for which the science is well-documented, followed by neurological and genetic measures if/when the international scientific foundation matures.

5.1.   Behavioral Science Data Collection and Analysis

The Task Force discovered many independent efforts at data collection, but found (save one, discussed below) no effort that was both comprehensive and aimed at sustained analysis. Serious cases of unacceptable behavior could probably have been avoided had important data not been "stovepiped" or had leaders and teammates been better educated on behavioral precursors. The two biggest gaps identified by the Task Force were:

1) Systematic and consolidated analyses of case studies to identify common behavioral factors and to establish a baseline for violent behavior in the military context, similar to what is routinely done in law enforcement agencies and workplace violence programs; and

2) Merging of key personnel data bases to identify "red flag" cases and/or support trend and effectiveness analyses of resiliency, intervention, or mitigation programs.

To address the first gap related to case studies, the approach should include the following:

- Consideration of a range of contextual, target, subject-level, and behavioral factors to estimate the risk of illicit targeted violence posed by a subject.

- Case analysis of suspected targeted violence cases, including near miss cases in internal DoD investigations.

- Comparison with cleared and known low-concern cases.

- An assessment of the reliability and validity of case study data collected from multiple sources.

- Determine whether the sampling techniques used in the broad spectrum of targeted violence cases address the heterogeneity of such events.

This case study effort should be integrated into implementation of the Threat Management Unit recommendation in this report. It should include systems and mechanisms for program evaluation and data analysis to identify targeted violence trends, review risk factors, and assist with training. Such program evaluation activity is also encouraged to assess the impact of threat management strategies utilized by already-established organizations. This evaluation should include potential impediments to the reporting of concerns, standards of practice elucidated through bystander reporting research performed in other contexts, and the success of DoD's outreach and education activity in promoting the reporting of legitimate concerns.

The second gap related to merged personnel data bases is starting to be addressed in a flagship program in the Army called the Research and Analysis Facilitation Team (RAFT). The intention of RAFT is to create the "Person Event Data Environment." It will bring together approximately 60 separate personnel databases in the Army, conduct its own analysis, and make the data (appropriately protected) available to researchers. As the system matures, the Task Force believes that there could be significant value derived in trend analysis to correlate the impact of resiliency programs (discussed in section 5.2) on violent behavior, as well as validation of case study risk factors across broader populations. A cautionary note is relevant regarding identification of "red flag" cases. One advantage of data analytics is the ability to handle large amounts of data which can then be applied to a model or template that subsequently identify instances when the data matches the model. At a minimum, this ability is contingent on access to data and a correct model/template. If properly constructed it helps "connect the dots". Data access is not guaranteed –data may exist in medical files, social networks, travel records, hobby centers, professional societies (e.g. the alleged anthrax letter perpetrator), work files – to name a few. In addition to data access issues, a model is not predictive. It is based on past behavior which can be manipulated by a perpetrator focused on accomplishing their plan. Predictive ability is often associated with data analytics but in this area the future is very murky regarding that particular capability.

5.2.   Resilience Training and Assessment Programs

The warfighting environment is rarely forgiving. This suggests the value of intervention before the threshold to, or transition across, the tipping point is reached, i.e., a "vaccination" instead of therapeutic approach. The best, and in many cases, only, tool today is keenly observant commanders and teammates. A more robust "vaccination" approach requires that we proactively reduce the stress level or prevent the transition to the tipping point. For example, can we better understand the threshold where environmental or personal degradation overtakes the ability to cope, i.e., better "see" an individual's tipping point coming? Can we link a tipping point to a behavioral outcome — depression, violence to self, violence to others? In other words, can we improve individual resiliency and avoidance of unacceptable behavioral outcomes? The Task Force's recommended "vaccination" approach is based on improving resiliency.

The Army, in particular, has recognized the value of such an approach by developing and implementing the ambitious Comprehensive Soldier Fitness (CSF) program for improving overall resiliency. This is a major step for the military in recognizing that psychological fitness is every bit as important as physical fitness. The four elements of the program are:

- Global Assessment Tool (GAT): an online self-assessment in the areas illustrated in Figure 6.

- Comprehensive Resilience Modules: online tailored training modules linked to GAT results for the individual.

- Institutional Military Resilience Training: school house training by the U.S. Army Training and Doctrine Command (TRADOC) at the unit level.

- Master Resilience Trainers: teachers of resilience skills to unit personnel and families located at unit and/or installation level.

Figure 6. Global Assessment Tool (GAT)

Although only two plus years into the program, the sanitized data from the GAT (i.e., not tied to individual identifiers) is providing correlating factors for suicides, violent crimes, and drug abuse. The data is also shedding light on who will or won't attrit early, leading to a potential psychological screening tool for recruits.

The Task Force also relied on previous DSB work, the 2010 Summer Study on Enhancing Adaptability of U.S. Military Forces,[18] to gain insight on training for resiliency in the warfighting environment. Excerpted below are findings and recommendations pertinent to this study and valid for resiliency training (referred to in that study as adaptability, but carrying the same meaning as we use here):

> "Long-standing service experience shows that appropriate training improves an individual's ability to cope with degraded military situations; in particular, the field of stress exposure training (SET) seeks to create training environments that are realistic enough to introduce the trainee to a range of possible stressors he/she is likely to encounter in the warfighting situation he/she is preparing to enter.[19] The three principles of stress training are:
>
> o Enhance familiarity with the task environment, to include the likely stressors and their effects;
> o Impart high performance skills, relevant to the particular stress environment; and
> o Practice skills and build confidence, but in a manner that allows gradual exposure to the stressful environment in order to build the trainee's confidence.

> "...training tends to be based on a general syllabus that calls for initial situations that are well ordered, progressing to increased disorder as the course proceeds. At the start, training improves basic skills, such as combat tactics, weapons proficiency, and situational awareness and assessment. This foundation enables clearing the mind to concentrate on dealing with the unanticipated. As the trainee moves toward more and more chaos, he or she eventually reaches failure. Training is designed to progress to the failure point gradually, based on the hypothesis that 'stress testing,' in ever more complex scenarios, induces learning and improves ability to cope with increasingly complex, disordered situations, i.e., to become more 'adaptable.'[20]...

> "One of the key questions asked in the SET community has been the effectiveness of the testing experience when the trainee subsequently experiences environments or events outside of the test environment. While the research is not extensive, it does indicate a positive correlation between stress exposure testing and the ability of the individual to cope effectively with unanticipated events in the warfighting environment.[21] Much more, however, remains to be learned about how to improve effectiveness and specificity of training to enhance inherent adaptability."

[18] Report of the Defense Science Board 2010 Summer Study on Enhancing Adaptability of U.S. Military Forces (Washington, DC: Defense Science Board, December 2010).

[19] Hancock and Szalma, Chapter 14. See also Cannon-Bowers, J.A. and Salas, E. (ed.), "Making Decision under Stress: Implications for Individual and Team Training," American Psychological Association, 1998.

[20] Friedland, N. and Keinan, G., "Training Effective Performance in stressful Situations: Three Approaches and Implications for Combat Training," Military Psychology, no.4, 1992; pp. 157-175.

[21] Gick, M.L. and Holyoak, K.J., "The Cognitive Basis of Knowledge Transfer," Transfer of Training: Contemporary Research and Applications, Academic Press, 1987, pp. 9-46; Schmidt, R. A. and Bjork, R.A., "New Conceptualization of Practice: Common Principles in Three Paradigms Suggest New Concepts for Training," Psychology Science, no. 3(4), 1992; pp. 207-217.

5.3. Biomarkers

There is a growing quest in behavioral research to measure and correlate measurable physiological, neural, and genetic biomarkers with behaviors, both observed and predicted. Understanding related to physiological biomarkers is more mature and recommended as an initial focus for DoD R&D. The other areas should be monitored closely as international research is extensive and making rapid progress. Appendix 14 summarizes biomarker research with a focus on the stress-response curve, physiological and neurochemical markers, and genomics.

While a "tipping point" at which performance deteriorates and maladaptive behavior is well established in stress-response research, rarely does that behavior, however personally maladaptive, become violent. There is clearly a behavioral and emotional instability and change at the tipping point but there are a number of directions that the outcome could take — escape and avoidance, psychological deterioration, alcohol or drugs, violence, and in some cases, more positive outcomes like determination and self-development. Another important question for future research concerns the individual and situational determinants of these outcome directions. If those are known, interventions become possible. Rather than trying to predict negative outcomes, and then intervene, however, this information may allow more optimal structural or contextual changes, training regimens (including resilience training), or other policies and/or programs that could be applied more broadly and improve the performance of all relevant personnel.

5.4. Recommendations

The Task Force believes that a positive, risk management approach best addresses the management of low probability, high consequence events such as targeted violent behavior. The most important factor in the transition of an individual's reaction past the tipping point appears to be the response to a critical combination of chronic and acute stress. On the positive side, however, acceptable performance can be correlated with resilience measures that include social connectivity, optimism, emotional fitness, trust, team work, and leadership. We hypothesize that these subjective measures can be correlated with quantitative markers: neuropsychological, neurophysiological, genetic, and neurochemical characteristics.

The simplest bottom line is that the predictive approach to human behavior is not useful for low probability/high consequence events, but the preventive approach is likely to be promising. We also believe that there are biomarkers that can be measured during well-controlled resilience training programs that would provide factual data to help to determine the stress/performance characteristics for individuals. We are therefore recommending a research program to determine subjective resilience measures derived from careful behavioral analysis and modeling, coupled in the long run to quantitative resilience biomarkers. The goal is to determine the tipping point for individuals to enable training to improve resiliency and to support intervention before a tipping point is reached.

Assistant Secretary of Defense (Research and Engineering) (ASD(R&E) should undertake a unified, but modest, effort to understand and test the performance of emerging tools, building on promising starts within and outside the DoD.

- In the near term, focus on conducting cases studies, resiliency training, and analyzing physiological biomarkers.
    - Collect and analyze behavioral science data in two domains:
        - Case studies of violent behavior – integrate behavioral indicators into implementation of TMU.
        - Follow and evaluate the Army's merger of personnel databases (initiated by the Army's Research and Analysis Facilitation Team (RAFT)); conduct trend and impact analysis.
    - Augment resilience training by identifying factors to improve effectiveness and specificity of training to enhance inherent adaptability.
        - Build on the Army's Comprehensive Soldier Fitness (CSF) program.
    - Biomarkers
        - Initiate biomarker-based measurement program to add "hard data," e.g. physiological measures, to the stress resiliency database.
        - Correlate physiological measurements with environmental factors to assess resiliency in the field.
        - Develop available rugged, miniaturized rapid diagnostics for battalion level use.
- Long-term: Biomarker Research and Development.
    - Monitor international research in the neurosciences and genomics as they relate to violent behavior.

6.0 Summary of Recommendations

Threat Management Near-Term Recommendations

The Secretary of Defense direct a Department-wide requirement for the Military Departments and DoD Agencies to establish a multidisciplinary TMU that identifies, assesses, and responds/manages threats of targeted violence.

- Designate an Executive Agent (EA) responsible for overseeing and managing the Department's TMUs. The EA would be responsible for management, oversight, identifying resources and training requirements, and serve as DoD's central point for threat management – with OSD policy oversight.

- Charter the Executive Agent to conduct operationally relevant research on the nature and extent of targeted violence affecting the DoD community in order to inform the operation of TMUs.

The designated Executive Agent should establish effective information sharing and communications among DoD TMUs and with appropriate non-DoD organizations:

- Establish an information sharing system that would facilitate the review and assessment of communications or behaviors of concern for immediate use by the TMUs and for analytic purposes.

- Develop and implement a communication strategy to establish a higher level of awareness regarding the risk of targeted violence throughout DoD. This should include methods of messaging to the DoD community and establishing multimodal response channels to optimize the capture of critical threat reports.

- Efforts dealing with targeted violence should take advantage of the significant overlap and be integrated as appropriate with related efforts including suicide prevention, impulsive violence, sexual harassment, early warning signs of Post-Traumatic Stress Disorder (PTSD), and coping with medical or financial stress, particularly with respect to the professional resources involved and associated training programs.

Information Sharing Recommendations

A. The General Counsel, collaboratively with other elements of the Department, develop clear and comprehensible guidance to provide better understanding to supervisors/ commanders of actual (as opposed to perceived) limitations on sharing of information:

- 1. Review the impact of privacy rules including those under the Privacy Act and HIPAA. If adverse impacts to the necessary flow of information are found, DoD should (1) take steps to mitigate those impacts, and, if found necessary (2) advance corrective legislative proposals.

- 2. DoD guidance (such as DoDI 1325.06, Handling Dissident and Protest Activity Among Military Members) should expressly state that religious speech or activities of a radical nature detrimental to DoD policy on conduct and behavior are not immunized from scrutiny merely by association with religious rhetoric or belief.

■ 3. Prepare concise, easily understood guidance on privacy and religious rules as they affect personnel actions and exchange of information on matters discussed in this report.

B. The Under Secretary of Defense for Intelligence and the Under Secretary of Defense for Policy, in coordination with the FBI, reassess DoD's current threat information sharing architecture both internal to the Department and externally with the goal of evaluating the migration of threat information down to the user level in a timely and thorough manner.

■ 1. As part of the assessment, DoD in collaboration with the FBI should develop a comprehensive, DoD-wide investigative database that would serve as a central repository of threat information. The database should be a collaborative endeavor ensuring all threat information is discoverable and accessible to trained threat management professionals experienced in sharing threat information with commanders and supervisors.

■ 2. Design a system of bench marks and metrics to be used to monitor and provide feedback from senior officials down to the user level on the effectiveness of information sharing practices and programs internal to the Department and with external partners.

C. The Department of the Army evaluate the organizational barriers that exist between INSCOM, CID and law enforcement and provide metrics to support current organizational constructs or develop new organizational constructs to improve the information flow.

Recommendations for Science and Technology

Assistant Secretary of Defense (Research and Engineering) (ASD(R&E)) should undertake a unified, but modest, effort to understand and test the performance of emerging tools, building on promising starts within and outside the DoD.

■ In the near term, focus on conducting cases studies, resiliency training, and analyzing physiological biomarkers.

  o Collect and analyze behavioral science data in two domains:

    ▪ Case studies of violent behavior – integrate behavioral indicators into implementation of TMU.

    ▪ Follow and evaluate the Army's merger of personnel databases (initiated by the Army's Research and Analysis Facilitation Team (RAFT)); conduct trend and impact analysis.

  o Augment resilience training by identifying factors to improve effectiveness and specificity of training to enhance inherent adaptability.

    ▪ Build on the Army's Comprehensive Soldier Fitness (CSF) program.

  o Biomarkers

- Initiate biomarker-based measurement program to add "hard data," e.g. physiological measures, to the stress resiliency database.
- Correlate physiological measurements with environmental factors to assess resiliency in the field.
- Develop available rugged, miniaturized rapid diagnostics for battalion level use.

■ Long-term: Biomarker Research and Development.

o Monitor international research in the neurosciences and genomics as they relate to violent behavior.

Appendix 1. Terms of Reference

THE UNDER SECRETARY OF DEFENSE
3010 DEFENSE PENTAGON
WASHINGTON, DC 20301-3010

ACQUISITION,
TECHNOLOGY
AND LOGISTICS

MAY 2 1 2011

MEMORANDUM FOR CHAIRMAN, DEFENSE SCIENCE BOARD

SUBJECT: Terms of Reference (TOR) – Defense Science Board (DSB) Task Force on Predicting Violent Behavior

Department of Defense (DoD) personnel are subject to a variety of practices to screen unwanted behavior. In general, the practices can be broken down into two broad categories: formal periodic checks and informal checks/observation related to routine interaction with supervisors, peers, and subordinates. Periodic checks conducted as part of the initial entry into the workforce, in support of security clearance investigations, and as suitability determinations for restricted programs are conducted in time scales often measured in years. Informal checks tend to occur on a daily basis as the individuals interact with their co-workers. Both types of checks miss a small number of individuals who engage in harmful behavior, either to themselves or to others in the workplace.

The Task Force will: examine and evaluate existing screening processes; and examine other governmental and non-governmental programs and best practices to establish standards, training, reporting requirements/mechanisms, and procedures for assessing predictive indicators relating to pending violence. When identifying pre-event behaviors, the Task Force will: focus on observable behavior that can be identified during a periodic check or in daily interaction; and investigate the potential applicability and efficacy of cyber behavior.

The Task Force should focus on the indicators leading to a wide range of destructive events, such as workplace violence, terrorism, and suicide. It should:

- Examine and evaluate existing screening programs to include those used in other branches of government (e.g., the Navy's Threat Management Unit and the Postal Service's "Going Postal Program"), private industry, and academia (e.g., Stanford University's workplace violence program) for successful programs and best practices. These may include efficacy of screening criteria, a decrease in time to conduct periodic checks, and potential advances in behavioral science and neurology.

  - Assess the adequacy of suitability criteria conducted in periodic checks and those provided to co-workers and supervisors. If current criteria are inadequate, suggest possible alternatives that are more effective given the large number of people involved and the range of activities requiring suitability determinations.

  - Evaluate the impact of the Privacy Act of 1974 and the Health Insurance Portability and Accountability Act, which prevent or inhibit real or perceived access to the official personnel or medical records of DoD members.

- Assess the network requirements and information flow, which could be used to correlate information across disparate sources, organizations, time frames, and geographic locations.

- Evaluate an organizational construct within the DoD to maximize effectiveness of current and future criminal and behavioral analysis and risk assessment capabilities and tools focused on an internal threat regardless of the target. Provide recommendations on best capabilities and tools for commanders/supervisors as the result of the assessment.

- Assess existing training and education programs to better assist DoD personnel in identifying potential aberrant behavior of violent actors.

The Task Force will provide an interim report to Assistant Secretary of Defense for Homeland Defense & Americas' Security Affairs (ASD(HD&ASA)) within 90 days of initiation and a final brief with findings and recommendations by June 30, 2011. The final report will be published within 90 days following completion of the brief out.

The Task Force will draw upon the full support of all Military Departments, DoD Components, Boards, Committees and Task Forces for information (including, but not limited to, documents and interviews of personnel) and analytical and investigative capacity as determined necessary by the Chairpersons of the Task Force.

The Task Force will be co-sponsored by the Under Secretary of Defense for Acquisition, Technology and Logistics and the Under Secretary of Defense for Policy. Ms. Judith Miller and Mr. Larry Lynn will serve as Co-chairpersons of the Task Force. Colonel Valrica Dunmyer, U.S. Army, Office of the Under Secretary of Defense for Policy, will serve as Executive Secretary, and Major Michael Warner, U.S. Air Force, will serve as the DSB Secretariat Representative. The ASD(HD&ASA) is authorized to act upon the advice and recommendations of the Board.

This Task Force will operate in accordance with the provisions of Public Law 92-463, the "Federal Advisory Committee Act," and DoD Directive 5105.04, the "DoD Federal Advisory Committee Program." It is not anticipated that this Task Force will need to go into any "particular matters" within the meaning of title 18, United States Code, section 208, nor will it cause any member to be placed in the position of acting as a procurement official.

Ashton B. Carter

2

Appendix 2. Task Force Membership

Co-Chairs

Mr. Larry Lynn	Private Consultant
Ms. Judith Miller, Esq	Private Consultant

Members

Dr. Gary Berntson	Ohio State University
Det. Jeff Dunn	Los Angeles Police Department
Mr. Rick Dunn	Private Consultant
Dr. Stephen Fienberg	Carnegie-Mellon University
Dr. Michael Gelles	Deloitte Consulting LLP
Dr. Christopher Green	Wayne State School of Medicine
Dr. Miriam John	Private Consultant
Dr. Mario Scalora	University of Nebraska-Lincoln
Dr. Anna Marie Skalka	Fox Chase Cancer Center
Dr. Lydia Thomas	Private Consultant
Dr. Gerry Yonas	Mind Research Network

Government Advisors

Ms. Christine Bader	OASD (Health Affairs)
Dr. Kelley Brix	OASD (Health Affairs)
Mr. Wade Ishimoto	Department of the Navy
Dr. Mark Maybury	Department of the Air Force
Mr. RC Porter	Defense Intelligence Agency
SSA Andre Simons	Federal Bureau of Investigation
Agent Dorian Van Horn	Naval Criminal Investigative Service

Senior Reviewer

Dr. Ted Gold	Private Consultant

Executive Secretary

COL Valrica Dunmyer, USA	OSD (Policy)

DSB Secretariat

Mr. Brian Hughes	Defense Science Board
Lt. Col. Michael Warner, USAF	Defense Science Board
CDR Doug Reinbold, USN	Defense Science Board

Support

Ms. Tammy-jean Beatty	SAIC
Ms. Amely Moore	SAIC
Mr. Jason Wood	SAIC

Appendix 3. Briefings Received

April 19-20, 2011		
Standards of Conduct Briefing and Swearing-In of DSB Members	Mr. Jeff Green	DoD Office of the General Counsel
Behavioral Science Insider Threat Research Program	Ms. Deborah Loftis	DIAC WG
Identifying Indications and Warnings of Insider Threat	Mr. Adam Cummings	CERT
Commercial Fraud Detection	Mr. John Ellingson	Skeptical Systems
DARPA ADAMS Program	Dr. Rand Waltzman	DARPA/ I2O
NAS Study on Polygraphs and Other Related Technologies?	Dr. Stephen Fienberg	Carnegie Mellon University
Workplace Violence/Insider Threat	Dr. Harley Stock	Incident Management Group, Inc
State of the Art in Non-invasive Neurological Observations	Dr. Steven Laken	Cephos Corp.
Threat Assessment and Management	Maj E.R. (Gene) Deisinger, PhD	Virginia Tech
May 23-24, 2011		
Insider Threat Challenge ARDA/IARPA	Dr. Mark Maybury	United States Air Force
NCIS Threat Management Unit	Ms. Dorian Van Horn	NCIS
LAPD Threat Management Unit	Det. Jeff Dunn	LAPD
Workplace Assessment of Violence Risk (WAVR-21)	Dr. Reid Meloy & Dr. Steve White	Work Trauma Services Inc.
Anticipating Aberrant Behavior: A (Former) P&R Perspective	Dr. David Chu	IDA
Skeptical Systems' Response to Task Force Questions	Mr. John Ellingson	Skeptical Systems
Individual Radicalization Process	Dr. Gary Ackerman	National Consortium for the Study of Terrorism and Responses to Terrorism
Preventing Targeted Violence by	Dr. Robert Fein	The Metis Group, Inc.

Lone Offenders: Ideas to Consider		
The Future Attribute Screening Technologies (FAST) Program	Dr. Dan Martin	MRAC LLC

June 14-15, 2011		
Air Force Suicide Prevention Program	Maj Michael McCarthy, USAF	United States Air Force
Marine Corps Suicide Prevention Program	Lt. CDR. Andrew Martin, USMC	United States Marine Corps
Navy Suicide Prevention Program	Lt. CDR. Bonnie Chavez, USN	United States Navy
Predicting Violent Behavior	Mr. Bryan Ware	Digital Sandbox
Insider Threat, Workplace Violence	Dr. Marc Sageman	Sageman Consulting LLC
DoD Personnel Reliability Program (PRP)	LCDR Thomas Whitehead, USN	OASD(NCB/NM)
Improving Assessments of Personality Disorders that are Security & Safety Risks	Eric L. Lang, Ph.D	Defense Personnel Security Research Center (PERSEREC)

July 20-21, 2011		
Behavioral Analysis Through the Interpretation of Facial Micro-expressions	Dr. Paul Ekman	Paul Ekman Group, LLC
Down in the Trenches: Operational Psychology and Insider	COL Sally Harvey, USA	INSCOM
Threat Information Sharing Working Group	Mr. Michael Rascati	OUSD(I)
Army Actions to Date Regarding Military Personnel Records	MAJ Sean Malik, USA	Army G-34 Protection Directorate
Virtual Secure Enclave Security Resiliency Program - Addressing the Insider Threat	Mr. Howard Hagan	Army G-2X
Air Force TMU	Mr. Daniel McGarvey	United States Air Force
FBI TMU	SSA Andre Simons	FBI
Confidentiality of Mental Health Records in the Military	Mr. John Casciotti	DoD Office of the General Counsel

August 25-26, 2011		
Insider Threat Working Group	Mr. Steve Knight	OADS(HDS&FP)
DoD Efforts to Get to an Integrated	Mr. John Awtrey	OUSD(P&R)

Law Enforcement Database		
PTSD	Dr. Charles Hoge	Division of Psychiatry and Neuroscience, Walter Reed Army Institute of Research
Ft. Hood Senior Steering Group	Hon. Todd M. Rosenblum, PDASD	ASD(HD&ASA)
Joint Staff Personnel Working Group	CAPT Kristin Strong, USN	Human Capital Division, J1, Manpower and Personnel Directorate
Marine Mindfulness-based Mind Fitness Training	Dr. Chris Johnson, Dr. Clarke Lethin Dr. Karl Van Orden	Naval Health Research Center
September 20-21, 2011		
The Privacy Act: Implications for Predicting Violent Behavior	Mr. Adam Sutton	DoD Office of the General Counsel
Dynamics of Machine Prediction, Preparedness, and Resiliency	Mr. Jeff Jonas, Chief Scientist	IBM Entity Analytics
October 18-19, 2011		
Detecting Deception	Dr. Andy Morgan	Yale University
Updated Threat Briefing	COL Sally Harvey, USA	INSCOM
Postal Service Threat Management and the Employee Assistance Program	Dr. Deborah Atkins	United States Postal Service
Religious Accommodation and Predicting Violent Behavior	Mr. Jim Schwenk	DoD Office of the General Counsel
DARPA R&D Initiatives	Dr. William Casebeer	DARPA/DSO
Commanders Panel	CAPT Mary M. Jackson, USN	Commanding Officer, Naval Station Norfolk
Commanders Panel	Col. Daniel J. Lecce, USMC	Base Commander, MCB Camp Lejeune
Commanders Panel	COL William A. Turner, USA	HQDA DCS G-3/5/7
November 8-9, 2011		
Comprehensive Solider Fitness Program	CPT Paul B. Lester, Ph.D, USA	Comprehensive Soldier Fitness Office, HQDA G-3/5/7
Psychological and Physiological Correlates of Loneliness	Dr. Louise Hawkley	Social Neuroscience Laboratory, University of Chicago

Appendix 4. Responses to Terms of Reference Tasking

1) *Examine and evaluate existing screening programs to include those used in other branches of government (e.g., the Navy's Threat Management Unit and the Postal Service's "Going Postal Program"), private industry, and academia (e.g., Stanford University's workplace violence program) for successful programs and standards of practice. These may include efficacy of screening criteria, a decrease in time to conduct periodic checks, and potential advances in behavioral science and neurology.*

Over the course of 8 two-day meetings focused on information gathering, the Task Force received numerous briefings from across government, private industry, and academia on existing screening programs. A complete listing of the briefings received by the Task Force can be found in Appendix 3.

- The programs presented to – and evaluated by – the Task Force were varied in scope. The range of targeted behaviors included workplace violence (USPS), school violence (Virginia Tech), suicide (Service prevention programs), homicide (LAPD, FBI/BAU), espionage/counter intelligence threats (DoE/NNSA), terrorism/radicalization (START), and cyber behavior (Digital Sandbox, Skeptical Systems, Inc.).

- Some of the programs examined by the Task Force were focused on developing technological solutions to screening for unwanted behavior (DARPA, Cephos). Other programs took a social-behavioral approach to addressing potential violent acts, focusing on peer-to-peer vigilance and community reporting (NCIS, Meloy (WAVR-21)).

In evaluating existing screening programs, the Task Force considered a number of factors and key questions, including:

- What operational benefits have been realized to date? What benefits are expected to be realized over the next 2-3 years, 5 years, or 10-plus years?

- Is a program or approach optimized to one particular timeline or scale?

- What partner organizations have worked within the DoD, the broader USG, academia, private industry, and internationally?

A sample of some of the common questions posed by the Task Force to briefers is included in Appendix 5.

The combination of the briefings received and the responses to Task Force questions helped study participants develop recommendations for implementing a balanced approach to preventing targeted violence in the DoD community – one that weighs incidence, consequence, resources, and results.

TOR Task 1 – Preliminary Conclusions. Currently, science does not offer a reliable or feasible approach to predicting violent behavior. Behavioral approaches focused on mitigating risk, managing threats, and enhancing resiliency offer near-term solutions and proven standards of practice that should be standardized across the DoD community. Additionally, the Task Force found that the goal of "predicting violent behavior" casts an extremely wide net in an effort to detect the precursors of exceedingly rare events. A more appropriate and effective goal for enhancing safety throughout the DoD community would be *preventing targeted violence*.

2) *Assess the adequacy of suitability criteria conducted in periodic checks and those provided to co-workers and supervisors. If current criteria are inadequate, suggest possible alternatives that are more effective given the large number of people involved and the range of activities requiring suitability determinations.*

The Task Force assessed the full range of programs, analytical techniques, criteria, and technologies used to screen Service members and civilians on a periodic basis. These included OPM guidelines for granting security clearances, special protocols in place as part of the Personnel Reliability Program, recent guidance from the Services (ALDODACT 09/10), as well as polygraph and other credibility assessment methods.

Of special note is the DoD's Nuclear Personnel Reliability Program (NPRP). Initiated in the 1960's, the NPRP is a long standing program designed to select and retain only those personnel who are emotionally stable and physically capable and who have demonstrated reliability and professional competence to perform duties associated with nuclear weapons or nuclear command and control systems and equipment involved with DoD's nuclear weapons. The selection process includes drug and alcohol testing and psychological screening. There are many attributes of the NPRP which suggest it as a potential role model for a DoD wide screening program. First, it operates at the local command level. The NPRP structure incorporates several organizations that an individual is likely to deal with (e.g. medical and dental) and allows supervisors and co-workers who encounter the individual on a daily basis to make informed judgment on the mindset of the individual. For example, NPRP enables temporary decertification without incurring any stigma that may be associated with decertification in other programs (e.g. loss of a security clearance). Secondly, it was relatively large covering over 100,000 individuals at the height of the Cold War. Finally, NPRP is coupled with other procedures and policies which enhance its overall effectiveness (e.g. two man control procedures and inspections by external expert teams).

Despite its advantages, the NPRP is not well suited as a model for a DoD wide screening program for targeted violence. First and foremost, despite a rigorous screening system, NPRP permanently decertifies a measurable number of individuals. Recent data indicates a range from 1.7% in 2007 (310 of 16,498 enrolled) to over 7% in 2009 (1,230 of 15,786 enrolled) were permanently decertified. Permanent decertification can occur for any number of reasons (e.g. alcohol, drug, financial, voluntary, etc.) and does not imply that the individual is no longer of use to the Department nor should it be construed that the individual is at risk to conduct targeted violence. However, even a program as selective and as rigorous as the NPRP does not currently achieve a high enough success rate to screen out the very low incidence of targeted violence experienced by DoD. Contributing to this inability to precisely screen out undesirable behavior in a select group of individuals, a classified 2010 JASONS study on Nuclear Weapons Surety noted that the NPRP does not currently demonstrate the capability to analyze the data generated from the NPRP in any meaningful way. In addition, every individual screened for inclusion into the NPRP undergoes a Personnel Security Investigation (PSI). PSIs occur at set intervals of up to five years between investigations. The transition to targeted violence does take time but in most instances the transition is less than five years in length. Any system designed to use the PSI process must rely on an investigation periodicity of much less than five years and would overburden the current system. PSIs are also relatively expensive and would not lend itself to a low cost solution. Finally, the NPRP data is not a scientifically valid sample as it does not allow identification of false negatives or false positives. At best it demonstrates a range of results that suggest the difficulties in any inferential screening system.

> **TOR Task 2 – Preliminary Conclusions.** Overall, the Task Force concludes that no single screening method, checklist, or list of behavioral indicators/criteria can reliably predict violent behavior. From a scientific perspective, the network, data, and analysis capability required to detect (with low false-positive/negative) rare events with few, if any, technologically perceivable precursors, does not exist. However, by shifting the focus of screening programs away from prediction toward prevention, there are proven threat management standards of practice that have been widely implemented in the private sector and elsewhere in government. DoD should adopt and standardize these practices. A key principle of threat management is to avoid placing the general population in the role of investigator. Rather than disseminating a checklist or set of behavioral indicators widely throughout a community, the message conveyed to the public should be "see something, say something." In essence, if an observation causes a community member to question whether or not the observation should be reported, it should be reported. Once concerning behavior is reported, trained threat management professionals using standards of practice and standardized methodologies can evaluate the risk for violence and the need for intervention.

3) *Evaluate the impact of the Privacy Act of 1974 and the Health Insurance Portability and Accountability Act (HIPAA), which prevent or inhibit real or perceived access to the official personnel or medical records of DoD members.*

The Task Force received three briefings from the DoD Office of the General Counsel (OGC) related to this tasking. The first briefing addressed HIPAA requirements and special considerations affecting the releasability of Service members' health information and a Commander's access to a subordinate's health information. Study participants also received an OGC brief on the Privacy Act of 1974 and how the law permits or restricts use or release of personal information in a variety of contexts related to screening for objectionable behavior. OGC then briefed the Task Force on the topic of religious accommodation and conscientious objector status as they relate to individual radicalization and possible insider threats within the military.

Additionally, the Task Force was briefed by representatives of the Joint Staff Personnel Working Group (JSPWG) and the U.S. Army G-3/5/7 G-34 Protection Directorate on efforts to address recommendation 2.9 of the Fort Hood Independent Review Panel, which identified gaps in the visibility of personnel records information to Commanders and a lack of operational definitions related to screening for violent behavior.

> **TOR Task 3 – Preliminary Conclusions.** The Task Force concludes that HIPAA, the Privacy Act, and policies governing religious accommodation and conscientious objector status do not preclude effective threat management throughout the DoD community. Military commanders are afforded access to a broad range of otherwise protected confidential health information, provided specific criteria for release are satisfied. A major impediment to increasing visibility to commanders of relevant private information is a lack of awareness among the healthcare community and military leadership of the releasability of Service members' private information. Absent this awareness, providers and commanders often defer to caution and do not request or grant access to subordinates' private information.

4) *Assess the network requirements and information flow, which could be used to correlate information across disparate sources, organizations, time frames, and geographic locations.*

The briefings received on network requirements and information flow (DARPA,) were extremely valuable as the Task Force worked to understand both the scope and scale of predicting extremely rare, but nonetheless consequential, events. In particular, representatives from private industry (Skeptical Systems, Digital Sandbox, IBM) helped Members understand the network needed to capture and analyze indicators of potential violent behavior on a predictive basis. Additionally, the implications of information gathering on privacy and other civil rights was a matter of discussion.

> **TOR Task 4 – Preliminary Conclusions.** Predictive indicators of future violent behavior are often difficult to perceive (in terms of data) or non-existent entirely. For this reason, detection and prediction of these relatively rare events – with any measure of reliability (in terms of low false-positive/negative) – would essentially require persistent surveillance using as many data streams as possible with a similarly large-scale analysis apparatus. Assuming that such a capability does exist at some future date, the results would be expected to be low-confidence.

5) *Evaluate an organizational construct within DoD to maximize effectiveness of current and future criminal and behavioral analysis and risk assessment capabilities and tools focused on an internal threat regardless of the target.*

The Task Force was briefed by representatives from the Services, other government entities, the private sector, and academia on a variety of technological and behavioral approaches to predicting or preventing violent behavior and targeted violence. To ensure the operational relevance of any prospective recommendations, the Task Force convened a panel of mid/field-grade base commanders representing the Services (USA, USN, and USMC). During this session, the commanders offered their perspective on the feasibility of future program recommendations – particularly additional training requirements.

For reasons stated earlier, science and technological approaches to screening for violent behavior are not adequate to provide large-scale, reliable predictive capability. However, adopting a behavioral approach that emphasizes risk reduction, threat management, and resiliency can provide the DoD community with effective methods and procedures to prevent targeted violence that have already been standardized throughout much of the private sector and elsewhere in government.

> **TOR Task 5 – Preliminary Conclusions.** Threat Management Units (TMUs) are an effective operational framework for a behavioral approach to preventing targeted violence. Utilizing a wide aperture for community reporting of concerning behavior, trained multidisciplinary TMU professionals focus on evaluating risk, managing threats, and intervening where necessary. TMUs have met with success in a variety of settings, to include education, corporate environments, and government (particularly the Postal Service and Department of the Navy/NCIS). The safety and security of the DoD community would be enhanced by standardizing threat management procedures via the establishment of TMUs across the Services and DoD agencies.

6) *Provide recommendations on best capabilities and tools for commanders/supervisors as the result of the assessment.*

The focus in response to this task is the organization of TMUs (Chapter 3) and commander's understanding of real limitations imposed (as opposed to perceptions) by HIPAA and the Privacy Act.

> **TOR Task 6 – Preliminary Conclusions**. Better understanding of the actual limitations will allow adequate information sharing.

7) *Assess existing training and education programs to better assist DoD personnel in identifying potential aberrant behavior of violent actors.*

The Task Force received numerous briefings from the private sector, government, and academia on innovative training and education programs to aid in identifying potential violent offenders and preventing targeted violence. These included analysis of facial micro-expressions, interpreting behavioral risk assessments, mindfulness-based mind fitness training, and credibility assessment.

More broadly, the Task Force was briefed on ongoing research efforts that are working to gather data on the mental resilience and fitness of the DoD community as a whole (Comprehensive Soldier Fitness Program/Global Assessment Tool) and how this data will be of use going forward. Additionally, each Service provided the Task Force with information and a briefing on suicide prevention programs and training initiatives currently in place or under development.

Finally, the panel of base commanders provided valuable operational perspective on the feasibility and utility of implementing a wide-spread violence prevention training requirement across the Services.

TOR Task 7 – Preliminary Conclusions. Many violence prevention education/training programs provide target populations with a checklist of troubling behaviors or warning signs. The public then compares observed behavior to these lists/criteria in order to determine what does or does not cross a threshold for reporting concerning behavior to authorities or supervisors. At least initially, this approach places the public in the role of investigator and relies on imperfect lists to capture highly subjective and contextual behaviors that may or may not indicate potential for violence. In addition, formal education and training of this type frequently becomes yet another administrative box to check among a myriad of other annual training requirements, providing little operational value. Going forward, the threat management approach to preventing targeted violence should emphasize wide-aperture, multi-modal reporting of *concerning behavior* generally (as opposed to a list of specific behaviors) by the DoD community. This report would then be formally evaluated by a multidisciplinary team of threat management professionals.

Appendix 5. Briefer Questionnaire

Broad Questions of Interest to the Task Force – regardless of briefers' specialty.

Based on your own sense of your field/program/research, what operational benefits can be realized over the next 2-3 years, 5 years, and 10-plus years?

- What level-of-effort (in terms of funding) would be required to realize these operational benefits according to the above time scales?

Is your particular approach to predicting violent behavior/insider threats optimized to one particular timeline (scope) or level of severity (scale)? For example: immediate threats of a tactical nature (targeted violence) or more strategic threats that may unfold over a period of years (sabotage).

- If so, what are the limits to your focus and at what point should alternative approaches be considered to address threats beyond the intended reach of your specialty/expertise?

What partner organizations have you engaged to date – particularly within DoD, but also more broadly within the USG, academia, private industry, and internationally?

What are the legal, moral, and ethical concerns raised by your approach to predicting violent behavior/insider threats?

Has any effort been made to formally assess statutory limitations that could impact your desired framework/approach (i.e. HIPAA, FERPA, Privacy Act)?

Balancing Approaches: Achieving the Appropriate Combination of S&T and Socio-Cultural Vigilance

Can S&T approaches to predicting violent behavior/insider threats be augmented by socio-cultural approaches? If so, how and to what degree?

Are certain approaches better suited to particular threat scenarios than others? For example, would a social-cultural (i.e. Wingman Program or Human Factors Board) approach be better suited to detecting and mitigating tactical threats – like targeted violence – in the days and weeks immediately preceding a violent incident than, say, a large-scale S&T screening or data-mining program? Or conversely, would something like the Wingman Program be poorly suited to uncovering advanced, meticulous strategic level threats that may develop over a period of years?

- If these approaches are not mutually exclusive, what is the right balance? How can DoD implement a program that optimally utilizes different approaches to address widely varying threats?

Can you provide insight on the potential for technology to help predict violent behavior/insider threats?

- In particular, we are interested in learning about the uses of biomarkers, clinical data, and actuarial data to identify potential violent offenders or threats.

- What are the network/sensor requirements for generating high-quality, low false-positive data? If we are unable to reliably predict incidents based on the available data (particularly in light of the low base rate of incidents), how can we quantify uncertainty and to what end?

Can you provide insight on the potential for socio-cultural efforts/human vigilance to help predict violent behavior/insider threats?

- Here too, we are concerned about the consequences of high false positives. What practical steps can be taken to ensure that insider threat detection mechanisms/programs are trusted, reliable, and confidential? Assuming that some false positives will occur, what steps can be implemented to minimize the consequences of these cases.

Calibrating Incidence, Consequences, and Investment.

The Task Force is currently discussing how to balance systems/technology-based solutions with a more socio-cultural approach to insider threat detection and mitigation. As part of this discussion, members are particularly interested in determining the appropriate level-of-effort for addressing the problem.

- Specifically, what degree of investment will be required to deploy sufficient resources to detect these exceedingly rare although high-impact, high politicized events – and more importantly, is this investment wise, given a) the low base rate of incidents; and b) the reliability/quality of the prediction capability that can be achieved?

- If – given a low base rate of occurrence – the level-of-effort is too great and/or the quality of prediction capability too low to justify major R&D, training and personnel commitments, what is the role of emergency preparedness and resiliency in a consequence management strategy?

Defining Terms and Evaluating Current Baseline Behavioral Indicators

In lieu of specific guidance on definitions related to predicting violent behavior/insider threats, DoD is currently relying on the Adjudicative Guidelines for Determining Eligibility for Access to Classified Information as a source for behavioral indicators of potential violent behavior. What are your thoughts regarding the suitability of these criteria and how would you adjust the aperture for making threat/suitability determinations?

Do you advocate particular definitions for the following terms? If so, what is included/excluded and why?

- insider threat
- self radicalization
- high risk behavior
- internal threats to force protection

- targeted violence
- radicalization
- behavioral indicators
- internal force protection

Appendix 6. Concerning Behaviors (as distinguished from Behavioral Indicators)

The purpose of this list is not a check sheet for concerning behavior but rather a series of inputs to rational thinking.

Verbal Signs:

- Direct and indirect threats
- Threatening/harassing phone calls
- Recurrent suicide threats or actions
- Boasts of violent behavior or fantasies
- Frequent profanity

- Belligerence
- Challenging or intimidating statements
- Expresses feelings of victimization/hopelessness
- Blames others for problems at work

Physical/Behavioral Signs:

- Physical altercation/assault upon another person
- Destruction of property
- Physical intimidation
- Following/surveilling targeted individuals

- Deteriorating physical appearance and self-care
- Inappropriate weapon possession or use
- Poor work performance
- Withdrawal from others at work

Organizational Events:

- Job action or threatened job action
- Non-promotion
- Inadequate training
- Poor supervision
- Unfair workload distribution
- Inadequate rewards, compensation or acknowledgement
- Poor communication

- Lack of administrative support
- Politics
- Unfair shift assignments
- Unfair disciplinary practices
- Favoritism
- Poor leadership
- Lack of clarity about roles, expectations and responsibilities

Personal Events:

- Loss of personal relationship
- Financial loss
- Legal action

- Loss of face or humiliation
- Significant personal rejection

Appendix 7. Example Entities that Operate TMUs

Listed below are example entities that operate TMUs.

Public/Government:

- Los Angeles Police Department
- Los Angeles County Sheriff's Department
- Los Angeles City Attorney's Office
- San Jose Police Department
- San Diego County District Attorney's Office
- California Highway Patrol
- Maricopa County Sheriff's Department
- Lincoln Police Department (Nebraska)
- Nebraska State Patrol

- NCIS
- FBI
- CIA
- DHS-FPS
- US Supreme Court
- US Postal Service
- Veteran's Affairs OIG
- US Capitol Police
- US Secret Service
- NYPD

Higher Education:

- University of Nebraska-Lincoln
- Iowa State University
- Pepperdine University
- University of Iowa
- Auburn University
- Georgia Tech
- Texas A&M

- Penn State
- Georgetown University
- George Mason University
- Virginia Tech
- University of Virginia
- Virginia Commonwealth University
- University of North Carolina

Corporations:

- Microsoft
- Coca Cola

- Boeing
- Disney

Appendix 8. Threat Triage Questions

The Safe Schools Initiative, a joint collaborative project between the U.S. Secret Service and the U.S. Department of Education, derived key questions designed to give threat assessment professionals a roadmap for an inquiry or assessment. Those questions are:

1. What are the subject's motive(s) and goals?

2. Have there been any communications suggesting ideas or intent to attack?

3. Has the subject shown inappropriate interest in any of the following?
   - previous attacks or attackers;
   - weapons (including recent acquisition of any relevant weapon);
   - incidents of mass violence (terrorism, workplace violence, mass murderers).

4. Has the subject engaged in attack-related behaviors? These behaviors might include:
   - developing an attack idea or plan;
   - making efforts to acquire or practice with weapons;
   - casing, or checking out, possible sites and areas for attack;
   - rehearsing attacks or ambushes.

5. Does the subject have the capacity to carry out an act of targeted violence?

6. Is the subject experiencing hopelessness, desperation and/or despair?

7. Does the subject have a trusting relationship with at least one responsible adult?

8. Does the subject see violence as an acceptable—or desirable—or the only—way to solve problems?

9. Is the subject's conversation and "story" consistent with his or her actions?

10. Are other people concerned about the subject's potential for violence?

11. What circumstances might affect the likelihood of an attack?

Appendix 9. TMU-Related Legislation from Virginia

VIRGINIA ACTS OF ASSEMBLY -- CHAPTER

An Act to amend and reenact § 44-146.18 of the Code of Virginia and to amend the Code of Virginia by adding in Chapter 1 of Title 23 sections numbered 23-9.2:9, 23-9.2:10, and 23-9.2:11, relating to crisis and emergency management for public institutions of higher education. [H 1449]
Approved

Be it enacted by the General Assembly of Virginia:
1. That § 44-146.18 of the Code of Virginia is amended and reenacted and that the Code of Virginia is amended by adding in Chapter 1 of Title 23 sections numbered 23-9.2:9, 23-9.2:10, and 23-9.2:11 as follows:

§ 23-9.2:9. Institutional crisis and emergency management plan; review required.
The board of visitors or other governing body of each public institution of higher education shall develop, adopt, and keep current a written crisis and emergency management plan. Every four years, each institution shall conduct a comprehensive review and revision of its crisis and emergency management plan to ensure the plan remains current, and the revised plan shall be adopted formally by the board of visitors or other governing body. Such review shall also be certified in writing to the Department of Emergency Management. The institution shall coordinate with the local emergency management organization, as defined by § 44-146.16, to ensure integration into the local emergency operations plan.

§ 23-9.2:10. Violence prevention committee; threat assessment team.

A. Each public college or university shall have in place policies and procedures for the prevention of violence on campus, including assessment and intervention with individuals whose behavior poses a threat to the safety of the campus community.

B. The board of visitors or other governing body of each public institution of higher education shall determine a committee structure on campus of individuals charged with education and prevention of violence on campus. Each committee shall include representatives from student affairs, law enforcement, human resources, counseling services, residence life, and other constituencies as needed. Such committee shall also consult with legal counsel as needed. Once formed, each committee shall develop a clear statement of: (i) mission, (ii) membership, and (iii) leadership. Such statement shall be published and available to the campus community.

C. Each committee shall be charged with: (i) providing guidance to students, faculty, and staff regarding recognition of threatening or aberrant behavior that may represent a threat to the community; (ii) identification of members of the campus community to whom threatening behavior should be reported; and (iii) policies and procedures for the assessment of individuals whose behavior may present a threat, appropriate means of intervention with such individuals, and sufficient means of action, including interim suspension or medical separation to resolve potential threats.

D. The board of visitors or other governing body of each public institution of higher education shall establish a specific threat assessment team that shall include members from law enforcement, mental health professionals, representatives of student affairs and human resources, and, if available, college or university counsel. Such team shall implement the assessment, intervention and action policies set forth by the committee pursuant to subsection C.

E. Each threat assessment team shall establish relationships or utilize existing relationships with local and state law enforcement agencies as well as mental health agencies to expedite assessment and intervention with individuals whose behavior may present a threat to safety.

§ 23-9.2:11. First warning and emergency notification system required.

By January 1, 2009, the governing boards of each public institution of higher education shall establish a comprehensive, prompt, and reliable first warning notification and emergency broadcast system for their students, faculty, and staff, both on and off campus. Such system shall be activated in the case of an emergency and may rely on website announcements; email notices; phone, cellular phone, and text messages; alert lines; public address systems; and other means of communication. In addition, each institution shall designate individuals authorized to activate the warning system and provide such individuals with appropriate training for its use.

§ 44-146.18. Department of Emergency Services continued as Department of Emergency Management; administration and operational control; coordinator and other personnel; powers and duties.

A. The State Office of Emergency Services is continued and shall hereafter be known as the Department of Emergency Management. Wherever the words "State Department of Emergency Services" are used in any law of the Commonwealth, they shall mean the Department of Emergency Management. During a declared emergency this Department shall revert to the operational control of the Governor. The Department shall have a coordinator who shall be appointed by and serve at the pleasure of the Governor and also serve as State Emergency Planning Director. The Department shall employ the professional, technical, secretarial, and clerical employees necessary for the performance of its functions.

B. The State Department of Emergency Management shall in the administration of emergency services and disaster preparedness programs:

> 1. In coordination with political subdivisions and state agencies, ensure that the Commonwealth has up-to-date assessments and preparedness plans to prevent, respond to and recover from all disasters including acts of terrorism;
>
> 2. Conduct a statewide emergency management assessment in cooperation with political subdivisions, private industry and other public and private entities deemed vital to preparedness, public safety and security. The assessment shall include a review of emergency response plans, which include the variety of hazards, natural and man-made. The assessment shall be updated annually;

3. Submit to the Governor and to the General Assembly, no later than the first day of each regular session of the General Assembly, an annual executive summary and report on the status of emergency management response plans throughout the Commonwealth and other measures taken or recommended to prevent, respond to and recover from disasters, including acts of terrorism. This report shall be made available to the Division of Legislative Automated Systems for the processing of legislative documents and reports. Information submitted in accordance with the procedures set forth in subdivision 4 of § 2.2-3705.2 shall not be disclosed unless:

a. It is requested by law-enforcement authorities in furtherance of an official investigation or the prosecution of a criminal act;

b. The agency holding the record is served with a proper judicial order; or

c. The agency holding the record has obtained written consent to release the information from the State Department of Emergency Management;

4. Promulgate plans and programs that are conducive to adequate disaster mitigation preparedness, response and recovery programs;

5. Prepare and maintain a State Emergency Operations Plan for disaster response and recovery operations that assigns primary and support responsibilities for basic emergency services functions to state agencies, organizations and personnel as appropriate;

6. Coordinate and administer disaster mitigation, preparedness, response and recovery plans and programs with the proponent federal, state and local government agencies and related groups;

7. Provide guidance and assistance to state agencies and units of local government in developing and maintaining emergency management and continuity of operations (COOP) programs, plans and systems;

8. Make necessary recommendations to agencies of the federal, state, or local governments on preventive and preparedness measures designed to eliminate or reduce disasters and their impact;

9. Determine requirements of the Commonwealth and its political subdivisions for those necessities needed in the event of a declared emergency which are not otherwise readily available;

10. Assist state agencies and political subdivisions in establishing and operating training programs and programs of public information and education regarding emergency services and disaster preparedness activities;

11. Consult with the Board of Education regarding the development and revision of a model school crisis and emergency management plan for the purpose of assisting public schools in establishing, operating, and maintaining emergency services and disaster preparedness activities;

12. Consult with the State Council of Higher Education in the development and revision of a model institutional crisis and emergency management plan for the purpose of assisting public and private two-year and four-year institutions of higher education in

establishing, operating, and maintaining emergency services and disaster preparedness activities and, as needed, in developing an institutional crisis and emergency management plan pursuant to § 23-9.2:9;

13. Develop standards, provide guidance and encourage the maintenance of local and state agency emergency operations plans;

14. Prepare, maintain, coordinate or implement emergency resource management plans and programs with federal, state and local government agencies and related groups, and make such surveys of industries, resources, and facilities within the Commonwealth, both public and private, as are necessary to carry out the purposes of this chapter;

15. Coordinate with the federal government and any public or private agency or entity in achieving any purpose of this chapter and in implementing programs for disaster prevention, mitigation, preparation, response, and recovery;

16. Establish guidelines pursuant to § 44-146.28, and administer payments to eligible applicants as authorized by the Governor;

17. Coordinate and be responsible for the receipt, evaluation, and dissemination of emergency services intelligence pertaining to all probable hazards affecting the Commonwealth;

18. Coordinate intelligence activities relating to terrorism with the Department of State Police; and

19. Develop an emergency response plan to address the needs of individuals with household pets and service animals in the event of a disaster and assist and coordinate with local agencies in developing an emergency response plan for household pets and service animals.

C. The State Department of Emergency Management shall during a period of impending emergency or declared emergency be responsible for:

1. The receipt, evaluation, and dissemination of intelligence pertaining to an impending or actual disaster;

2. Providing facilities from which state agencies and supporting organizations may conduct emergency operations;

3. Providing an adequate communications and warning system capable of notifying all political subdivisions in the Commonwealth of an impending disaster within a reasonable time;

4. Establishing and maintaining liaison with affected political subdivisions;

5. Determining requirements for disaster relief and recovery assistance;

6. Coordinating disaster response actions of federal, state and volunteer relief agencies;

7. Coordinating and providing guidance and assistance to affected political subdivisions to ensure orderly and timely response to and recovery from disaster effects.

D. The State Department of Emergency Management shall be provided the necessary facilities and equipment needed to perform its normal day-to-day activities and coordinate disaster-related activities of the various federal, state, and other agencies during a state of emergency declaration by the Governor or following a major disaster declaration by the President.

E. The State Department of Emergency Management is authorized to enter into all contracts and agreements necessary or incidental to performance of any of its duties stated in this section or otherwise assigned to it by law, including contracts with the United States, other states, agencies and government subdivisions of the Commonwealth, and other appropriate public and private entities.

F. The State Department of Emergency Management shall encourage private industries whose goods and services are deemed vital to the public good to provide annually updated preparedness assessments to the local coordinator of emergency management on or before April 1 of each year, to facilitate overall Commonwealth preparedness. For the purposes of this section, "private industry" means companies, private hospitals, and other businesses or organizations deemed by the State Coordinator of Emergency Management to be essential to the public safety and well-being of the citizens of the Commonwealth.

Appendix 10. Action Memo

MEMORANDUM FOR: SEE DISTRIBUTION

SUBJECT: Implementation of a Department-wide Threat Management Capability to combat the Insider Threat

I am committed to ensuring a safe and secure environment for our men and women in uniform, their families and DoD Employees and Contractors. In the immediate aftermath of the November 2009 Fort Hood tragedy, Former Secretary Gates issued interim guidance on how to identify and report potential insider threats. The guidance served as a refresher to all on those behaviors that may indicate radicalization or a propensity for violence as well as appropriate procedures for reporting this behavior.

In May 2011, the Under Secretary of Defense for Acquisition, Technology, and Logistics and the Under Secretary of Defense for Policy chartered the Defense Science Board Task Force on Predicting Violent Behavior to examine other governmental and non-governmental programs and best practices to establish standards, training, reporting standards, and procedures for assessing indicators that could lead to violence.

The Task Force concluded its study after nine months of information gathering that included numerous briefings from experts in the various fields of study and unanimously agreed that the Department requires a shift from traditional methods of identifying and assessing those within our ranks that would do us harm. The current list of behavioral indicators as outlined in the interim guidance, while extensive, should not be used in isolation and as a single source for identifying individuals prone to violence.

I fully endorse and direct the implementation of the Task Force's information sharing and science and technology recommendations. Additionally, I endorse and direct the implementation of the Task Force's recommendation to adopt a Department-wide behavioral risk management standard that includes a multidisciplinary team of professionals led by credentialed law enforcement professionals trained in identifying, assessing, and managing behaviors of concern. These types of threat management teams exist today in academia, private industry, and other government sectors. While underrepresented in the Department, it would be a minimal undertaking that would yield high dividends in averting a reoccurrence of another Fort Hood incident.

The ASD(HD&ASA), previously tasked to lead the Fort Hood Follow-on Review, will ensure inclusion and implementation of this PVB TF's recommendation into the final report.

Attachments:

As stated

DISTRIBUTION:
SECRETARIES OF THE MILITARY DEPARTMENTS
CHAIRMAN OF THE JOINT CHIEFS OF STAFF
UNDER SECRETARIES OF DEFENSE
DEPUTY CHIEF MANAGEMENT OFFICER
CHIEFS OF THE MILITARY SERVICES
COMMANDANT OF THE COAST GUARD
CHIEF, NATIONAL GUARD BUREAU
COMMANDERS OF THE COMBATANT COMMANDS
ASSISTANT SECRETARIES OF DEFENSE
GENERAL COUNSEL OF THE DEPARTMENT OF DEFENE
DIRECTOR, OPERATIONAL TEST AND EVALUATION
DIRECTOR, COST ASSESSMENT AND PROGRAM EVALUATION
INSPECTOR GENERAL OF THE DEPARTMENT OF DEFENSE
ASSISTANTS TO THE SECRETARY OF DEFENSE
DIRECTOR, ADMINISTRATION AND MANAGEMENT
DIRECTOR, NET ASSESSMENT
DIRECTORS OF THE DEFENSE AGENCIES
DIRECTORS F THE DOD FIELD ACTIVITIES

Appendix 11. Privacy Act: Blanket Routine Uses

DoD BLANKET ROUTINE USES

NOTE: Information relating to, but not in and of itself constituting, terrorism, homeland security, or law enforcement information, as defined below, may only be disclosed upon a showing by the requester that the information is pertinent to the conduct of investigations of, or the development of analyses regarding, terrorism.

01. Law Enforcement Routine Use:

If a system of records maintained by a DoD Component to carry out its functions indicates a violation or potential violation of law, whether civil, criminal, or regulatory in nature, and whether arising by general statute or by regulation, rule, or order issued pursuant thereto, the relevant records in the system of records may be referred, as a routine use, to the agency concerned, whether federal, state, local, or foreign, charged with the responsibility of investigating or prosecuting such violation or charged with enforcing or implementing the statute, rule, regulation, or order issued pursuant thereto.

02. Disclosure When Requesting Information Routine Use:

A record from a system of records maintained by a DoD Component may be disclosed as a routine use to a federal, state, or local agency maintaining civil, criminal, or other relevant enforcement information or other pertinent information, such as current licenses, if necessary to obtain information relevant to a DoD Component decision concerning the hiring or retention of an employee, the issuance of a security clearance, the letting of a contract, or the issuance of a license, grant, or other benefit.

03. Disclosure of Requested Information Routine Use:

A record from a system of records maintained by a DoD Component may be disclosed to a federal agency, in response to its request, in connection with the hiring or retention of an employee, the issuance of a security clearance, the reporting of an investigation of an employee, the letting of a contract, or the issuance of a license, grant, or other benefit by the requesting agency, to the extent that the information is relevant and necessary to the requesting agency's decision on the matter.

06. Disclosures Required by International Agreements Routine Use:

A record from a system of records maintained by a DoD Component may be disclosed to foreign law enforcement, security, investigatory, or administrative authorities to comply with requirements imposed by, or to claim rights conferred in, international agreements and arrangements including those regulating the stationing and status in foreign countries of DoD military and civilian personnel.

09. Disclosure to the Department of Justice for Litigation Routine Use:

A record from a system of records maintained by a DoD Component may be disclosed as a routine use to any component of the Department of Justice for the purpose of representing the Department of Defense, or any officer, employee or member of the Department in pending or potential litigation to which the record is pertinent.

14. Counterintelligence Purpose Routine Use:

A record from a system of records maintained by a DoD Component may be disclosed as a routine use outside the DoD or the U.S. Government for the purpose of counterintelligence activities authorized by U.S. Law or Executive Order or for the purpose of enforcing laws which protect the national security of the United States.

15. Data Breach Remediation Purposes Routine Use:

A record from a system of records maintained by a Component may be disclosed to appropriate agencies, entities, and persons when (1) The Component suspects or has confirmed that the security or confidentiality of the information in the system of records has been compromised; (2) the Component has determined that as a result of the suspected or confirmed compromise there is a risk of harm to economic or property interests, identity theft or fraud, or harm to the security or integrity of this system or other systems or programs (whether maintained by the Component or another agency or entity) that rely upon the compromised information; and (3) the disclosure made to such agencies, entities, and persons is reasonably necessary to assist in connection with the Components efforts to respond to the suspected or confirmed compromise and prevent, minimize, or remedy such harm.

16. Information Sharing Environment Routine Use:

A record from a system of records maintained by a Component consisting of, or relating to, terrorism information (6 U.S.C. 485(a)(4)), homeland security information (6 U.S.C. 482(f)(1)), or Law enforcement information (Guideline 2 Report attached to White House Memorandum, "Information Sharing Environment, November 22, 2006) may be disclosed to a Federal, State, local, tribal, territorial, foreign governmental and/or multinational agency, either in response to its request or upon the initiative of the Component, for purposes of sharing such information as is necessary and relevant for the agencies to the detection, prevention, disruption, preemption, and mitigation of the effects of terrorist activities against the territory, people, and interests of the United States of America as contemplated by the Intelligence Reform and Terrorism Protection Act of 2004 (Public Law 108-458) and Executive Order 13388 (October 25, 2005).

Appendix 12. HIPAA

The Health Insurance Portability and Accountability Act (HIPAA) Privacy Rule (45 CFR 164.512(k)) establishes the standard for uses and disclosures of protected health information for specialized government functions, including Armed Forces personnel:

"A covered entity may use and disclose the protected health information of individuals who are Armed Forces personnel for activities deemed necessary by appropriate military command authorities to assure the proper execution of the military mission, if the appropriate military authority has published by notice in the Federal Register the following information:

(A) Appropriate military command authorities; and
(B) The purposes for which the protected health information may be used or disclosed."

"A covered entity that is a component of the Departments of Defense or Transportation may disclose to the Department of Veterans Affairs (DVA) the protected health information of an individual who is a member of the Armed Forces upon the separation or discharge of the individual from military service for the purpose of a determination by DVA of the individual's eligibility for or entitlement to benefits under laws administered by the Secretary of Veterans Affairs."

DoD 6025.18-R implements 45 C.F.R. 164.512(k) allowing DoD personnel to access medical information consistent with the controlling HHS regulation.

DoD 8580.02 establishes responsibilities and policies for securing and protecting health information of DoD personnel.

Appendix 13. Prediction: Why It Won't Work

As noted in Chapter 5, low base-rate events with high consequence pose a management challenge. Events such as nuclear accidents, earthquakes and tsunamis, or Ft Hood-type incidents do not lend themselves to prediction, so it is often not apparent when specific focal interventions, such as evacuations or psychological interventions, should be pursued. Rather, more meaningful management efforts would likely entail broader management strategies, such as maintenance plans for nuclear facilities or parallel efforts to mitigate psychological stressors. Although there may be predictor variables available in the above scenarios, they often provide only an increment in stochastic probability rather than a prediction certain. In targeted violence, for example, there may be pre-existing behavior markers that are specifiable. While such markers may be sensitive, they are of low specificity and thus carry the baggage of an unavoidable false alarm rate, which limits feasibility of prediction-intervention strategies. A more viable approach, therefore, may be the identification of individual, including cognitive, emotional and motivational variables, as well as contextual determinants of targeted violence. This would allow the establishment of management plans and mitigation efforts that could be applied broadly and may reduce the incidence of such negative outcomes. This represents a prevention rather than a prediction focus.

The importance of focusing on prevention rather than prediction can be illustrated with the following hypothetical example. Suppose we actually had a behavioral or biological screening test to identify those who are capable of targeted violent behavior with moderately high accuracy (something we in fact do not have at present). Table 4 represents the predictive accuracy of such a test applied in two modes – one aggressive and another more conservative – in a screening application to a hypothetical military base with a population of 10,000 military personnel. The population includes ten individuals with extreme violent tendencies, capable of executing an event such as that which occurred at Ft. Hood. In the aggressive mode, the test is strict enough to correctly identify 80% of those capable of extreme illicit violence. Accordingly, it identifies eight of ten individuals we wish to detect, but also falsely implicates 1,598 personnel who do not have these violent tendencies, i.e., who are "normal." Someone who "failed" this screening test would have a 99.5% chance of being normal, but we would have to invest enormous resources in further examining all 1,606 of those identified to find the eight bad apples, and currently we have no method for doing so. The damage this would inflict on the military base and its personnel is palpable. In the "conservative mode," the test protects the normal, non-violent personnel. Only about 39 personnel would fail the test, but eight of the ten extremely violent people would "pass" and be allowed to continue on to potentially act out their aggressions and commit a truly violent act, another Ft. hood incident-- with the attendant damage we set out to prevent.

Table 4 shows the expected results of screening for violent behavior with better than state-of-the-art accuracy at a hypothetical military base with a population of 10,000 military personnel that includes ten individuals with extreme violent tendencies.

Table 4. Expected Results of Screening for Violent Behavior

Examinee's True Condition	Violent	Non-Violent	Total
(A) Aggressive screening mode: Test set to detect great majority (80%) of personnel with extreme violent tendencies.			
"Fail"	8	1,598	1,606
"Pass"	2	8,392	8,394
Total	10	9,990	10,000
(B) Conservative mode: Test set to protect those not exhibiting violent tendencies.			
"Fail"	2	39	41
"Pass"	8	9,951	9,959
Total	10	9,990	10,000

We cannot overemphasize that there is no scientific basis for a screening instrument to test for future targeted violent behavior that is anywhere close to being as accurate as the hypothetical example above. Although scientific research does not allow a precise determination of how much less accurate any current detection instrument may be, any such instrument would nevertheless falsely identify even more individuals in the "aggressive mode" and fail to detect the truly violent individuals in the "conservative mode."

Appendix 14. Biomarkers in Research and Literature

The Stress-Response Curve. There is now over a hundred years of literature on the effects of arousal and stress on cognitive function and performance. Although different models and perspectives have emerged, there is a pervasive thread that extends across this literature. Specifically, there appears to be an optimal level of arousal/stress for efficient psychological processing. In 1908, Robert Yerkes and John Dodson formulated what has become known as the Yerkes-Dodson Law, which stipulates that performance increases with increasing mental or physical arousal up to a point, and then deteriorates with further levels of arousal.[22] The optimal point varies with the complexity or demands of the task (simpler tasks show a higher arousal-performance maxima) and varies from individual to individual. This general model has been extended to the stress-performance relationship.[23] Again, stress can enhance performance up to a point, but at higher levels becomes disruptive. This disruption can motivate a variety of outcomes, including in a few tragic cases, targeted violence.

The literature also documents considerable individual differences in the susceptibility to stress and in resilience in the face of stress. Blascovich & Tomaka (1996) outlined an influential appraisal model of stress reactivity that posits two basic modes of appraisal of a stress or other task demand-- challenge and threat.[24] A challenge appraisal entails an evaluation by the subject that he/she has sufficient skills and resources (intellectual, emotional, motivational, physical, etc.) to deal with the stress or accomplish the task. In contrast, a threat appraisal ensues if the person perceives he/she does not have the requisite skills and resources. Challenge appraisals are associated with more optimal performance and more adaptive responding, whereas threat appraisals are more likely associated with poorer performance or even freezing, narrowing of attentional focus, and avoidance.

Physiological Markers. Importantly, these appraisal states are not limited to the psychological domain, but become embodied in distinct patterns of cardiovascular response. Challenge appraisals are associated with cardiac sympathetic mobilization (increased stroke volume and cardiac output, which optimizes cardiovascular performance and circulation), whereas threat appraisals are associated with vasoconstriction (increased total peripheral resistance and blood pressure, which compromises circulation). This is an important finding which documents that adaptive and maladaptive responses to stress manifest in distinct patterns of physiological response. It suggests that measurements of such factors, if they can be made practical, might allow interventions prior to a tipping point.

---

[22] See also Wickens and Hollands: Wickens, C. .D & Hollands, J. G. (2000). *Engineering Psychology and Human Performance*, Prentice- Hall Inc., 2000, pp. 480-492.

[23] See Stall: Staal, M. A., "Stress, Cognition, and Human Performance: A Literature Review and Conceptual Framework." 2004 *NASA/TM—2004–212824* located at http://human-factors.arc.nasa.gov/flightcognition/Publications/IH_054_Staal.pdf ; for specific relevance to the military see Hancock, P.A. & Szalma, J. L. (Eds). "Performance Under Stress" *Human Factors in Defence*, Ashgate Publishing Lmt, Hamshire England, 2008.

[24] Blascovich, J., & Tomaka, J., "The biopsychosocial model of arousal regulation." *Advances in Experimental Social Psychology (Vol. 28, pp. 1-51)*, 1996 New York: Academic Press; See also Blascovich J, Mendes WB, Tomaka J, Salomon K, Seery M.,"The robust nature of the biopsychosocial model challenge and threat: a reply to Wright and Kirby," Pers Soc Psychol Rev. 7, 2003, pp. 234-243.

<u>Neurochemical Markers</u>. In parallel with the largely behavioral research outlined above, it is important to maintain active investigation of neurochemical and other biomarkers, not only as potential indicators of violence, but as markers of important nodal points in the pathway toward violence. For example, the inverted U stress-performance level is paralleled by cortisol levels, which may serve as an indicator of the tipping point in threat-challenge appraisals or in levels of stress (Lupien et al., 2007).

<u>Genomics</u>. Genomics as a screening tool to predict proclivity for violence, especially in military personnel, is starting to receive attention. While it is possible that an aggregated set of behavioral indicators may be useful in the near-term, the most well-known and now largest area of research in behavioral prediction (Neuroeconomics / Genomics Biomarkers) is not thought to be of near term utility. This was supported by a major effort initiated by STRATCOM, JS/J3/DDGO, OSD/DDRE/RRTO, and DARPA, NIH, CIA, DIA, DRDC, and in conjunction with the DOJ, NSF, and OSTP to search for biomarkers specifically related to the *Prediction of Political Violence* and to review current State-of-Research programs, including those from Universities sponsored by DoD. The results were presented in a two-day NIH workshop in 2010. Although the workshop focused on political violence, there is considerable relevance for the present concern of targeted violence.

Genomics together with a set of additional biochemical markers could have utility under special circumstances. Required, however, is a condition where other clinical medical and behavioral data showing a proclivity for violent acts, based on epidemiological and demographic-population data. In each of these cases, the attempt is being made to discover genomic predictors, useful for eventual screening of large populations who have been identified as high risk due to social indicators for violent acts.

No current medical or behavioral group in the DoD is actively following the notion of genomics as a biomarker family of predictors for proclivity for violent acts, with or without ancillary social conditions as triggers. The Task Force believes that this fragile and controversial area needs maturation and development in the broader academic community, to identify the most promising areas of future work. DoD should follow current research as a hedge against discovery, but a DoD unique research program is not warranted at this time.

<u>Considerations for Resiliency Training</u>. Although there are trait-like individual differences in the likelihood of threat vs. challenge appraisals, and there may be some genetic contribution to this, these dispositions are not immutable. Indeed, education and skill training can buffer individuals from threat modes of response. Moreover, even cognitive re-framing of the task or stressor, which is trainable, may shift the mode of response. Skinner and Brewer (2002), for example, found that viewing an event as challenging rather than threatening generally results in improved emotion-coping styles, positive feelings, and greater confidence. This may be a critical target for resilience training. As such, we recommend that the Department:

1) Augment resilience training and assessment programs to measure key stress contributors (e.g., sleep, personal connectedness) and effectiveness of resiliency training regimens.

2) Develop a modest research program to determine subjective resilience measures derived from careful behavioral analysis and modeling, coupled in the long run to quantitative resilience biomarkers. The goal is to determine the tipping point for individuals to enable training to improve resiliency and to support intervention before a tipping point is reached.

3) Collect neurophysiology data during the soldier fitness training program in order to provide a scientific basis for prevention of violent behavior.

Appendix 15. Definitions

Definitions

Insider threat:
A person, known or suspected, who uses their authorized access to Department of Defense facilities, systems, equipment, information or infrastructure to damage, disrupt operations, commit espionage on behalf of a foreign intelligence entity or support international terrorist organizations. (JP 2-01.2)

Internal force protection: Preventive measures taken to mitigate hostile actions against Department of Defense personnel (to include family members), resources, facilities, and critical information. Also called FP. (JP1-02)

Targeted violence: Pre-conceived violence focused on individuals, groups, or locations where perpetrators are engaged in behaviors that precede and are related to their attacks. These perpetrators consider, plan and prepare before engaging in acts of violence and are often detectable, providing an opportunity for disruption of the intended violence.[25] JP1-02 does not include a definition for targeted violence.

Self-radicalization: The process whereby people seek out opportunities for involvement in terrorist activity absent a formal involvement in a terrorist group and/or recruitment by others.[26] JP1-02 does not include a definition for self-radicalization.

Radicalization: The social and behavioral process whereby people adopt and embrace extremist attitudes, values or behaviors. It is a risk factor for involvement in terrorism, but involvement in terrorism does not always result from radicalization.[27] JP1-02 does not include a definition for radicalization.[28]

Self radicalization: A phenomenon in which individuals become terrorists without joining an established radical group, although they may be influenced by its ideology and message.

High risk behavior: nothing included in JP1-02.

Behavioral indicators: nothing included in JP1-02.

Internal threats to force protection: nothing included in JP1-02.

---

[25] As defined by Task Force member, Det. Jeff Dunn.
[26] As provided by Task Force member, Dr. Michael Gelles, citing Horgan's 2012 *The Psychology of Terrorism 2nd Edition*.
[27] Ibid.
[28] Hogan, M., 2012. *The Psychology of Terrorism 2nd Edition*.

Appendix 16. Acronyms

Acronyms	
Army G-2X	U.S. Army Counterintelligence, Human Intelligence, Security and Disclosure Directorate
ASD(HD&ASA)	Assistant Secretary of Defense for Homeland Defense & America's Security Affairs
ASD(R&E)	Assistant Secretary of Defense for Research and Engineering
ASIS	American Society for Industrial Security
AT	Antiterrorism
ATAP	Association of Threat Assessment Professionals
AWOL	Absent Without Leave
BAU	Behavioral Analysis Unit
BI	behavioral indicators
BTAC	Behavioral Threat Assessment Center
CID	U.S. Army Criminal Investigation Command
CONUS	Continental United States
CMG	Case Management Group
CSF	Comprehensive Solider Fitness program
CTAD	Communicated Threat Assessment Database
DARPA	Defense Advanced Research Projects Agency
DCHC	Defense Counterintelligence and Human Intelligence Center
DoD	Department of Defense
DoDD	Department of Defense Directive
DoD GC	DoD General Counsel
DoDI	Department of Defense Instruction
DSB	Defense Science Board
DSTL	Developing Science and Technology List

DV	Domestic Violence
DVA	Department of Veterans Affairs
DWP	Department of Water and Power
EA	Executive Agent
FAP	Family Advocacy Program
FBI	Federal Bureau of Investigation
GAT	Global Assessment Tool
HIPAA	Health Insurance Portability and Accountability Act
INSCOM	U.S. Army Intelligence and Security Command
J1	Joint Staff Manpower and Personnel Directorate
JP1-02	Joint Publication 1-02 Department of Defense Dictionary of Military and Associated Terms
JTTF	Joint Terrorism Task Force
LAPD	Los Angeles Police Department
LEO	Law Enforcement Officer
LHM	Letter Head Memorandum
MOU	Memorandum of Understanding
NCAVC	National Center for the Analysis of Violent Crime
NCIS	Naval Criminal Investigative Service
NCISHQ	Naval Criminal Investigative Service Headquarters
NJTTF	National Joint Terrorism Task Force
NPRP	Nuclear Personnel Reliability Program
OASD(HA)	Office of the Assistant Secretary of Defense for Health Affairs
OASD(HA/TMA)	Office of the Assistant Secretary of Defense for Health Affairs/TRICARE Management Activity
OASD(HD&ASA)	Office of the Assistant Secretary of Defense for Homeland Defense & America's Security Affairs
OCONUS	Outside the continental United States

OGC	Office of the General Counsel
OUSD(I)	Office of the Under Secretary of Defense for Intelligence
OMPF	Official Military Personnel File
OPM	Office of Personnel Management
PFC	Private First Class
PSI	Personnel Security Investigation
PTSD	Post-Traumatic Stress Disorder
PVB	Preventing Violent Behavior
R&D	research and development
RAFT	Research and Analysis Facilitation Team
S&T	science and technology
SAG	Senior Advisory Group
SECDEF	Secretary of Defense
SET	Stress Exposure Training
SSA	Supervisory Special Agent
SSG	Senior Steering Group
TAD	Temporary Assigned Duty
TAS	Threat Assessment Section
TAT	Threat Assessment Team
TF	Task Force
TMU	Threat Management Unit
TRADOC	U.S. Army Training and Doctrine Command
TOR	Terms of Reference
TV	Targeted Violence
UNL	University of Nebraska-Lincoln
USA	United States Army
USAF	United States Air Force

USD(AT&L)	Under Secretary of Defense for Acquisition, Technology, and Logistics
USD(I)	Under Secretary of Defense for Intelligence
USD(P&R)	Under Secretary of Defense for Personnel and Readiness
USD(P)	Under Secretary of Defense for Policy
USG	U.S. Government
USMC	United States Marine Corps
USN	United States Navy
WPV	Workplace Violence

Bibliography

Threat Assessment and Screening

Behavioral Intervention and Threat Assessment Policy. Dover, DE: Delaware Technical & Community College, January 2008. http://www.dtcc.edu/stanton/safety/threat_assessment_policy.pdf

Conner, Michael G. "An Internet-Based Screening Program for Mental Health Problems and the Risk of Violent, Suicidal and Self-Injuring Behavior." Portland, OR: Mentor Research Institute, March 18, 2006. http://www.mentorresearch.org/Documents/InternetScreeningForMentalHealthProblems.pdf

Dunkle, John H., et al. "Managing Violent and Other Troubling Students: The Role of Threat Assessment Teams on Campus." *Journal of College and University Law* Vol. 34 No. 3 (2008): 585-636. http://www.campusthreatassessment.org/images/uploads/instructor_resources/Dunkle_Warner_Silverstein_mep.pdf

Overview of Human Factors Behavioral Sciences Projects. Washington, DC: U.S. Department of Homeland Security, August 2009. http://www.dhs.gov/files/programs/gc_1218480185439.shtm

Randazzo, Marisa Reddy, et al. "Threat Assessment in Schools: Empirical Support and Comparison with Other Approaches." In S.R. Jimerson and M.J. Furlong, eds. The Handbook of School Violence and School Safety: From Research to Practice. Mahwah, NJ: Lawrence Erlbaum Associates, Inc., 2006. http://www.threatresources.com/downloads/LE140c10_p147-156.pdf

Review of *Danger Between the Lines: A Reference Manual for the Profiling of Violent Behavior* by Kimon S. Iannetta and James F. Craine. *The Forensic Examiner* (Summer 2009): 89.

Risk Assessment Guideline Elements for Violence: Considerations for Assessing the Risk of Future Violent Behavior. Sacramento, CA: Association of Threat Assessment Professionals, September 2006. http://downloads.workplaceviolencenews.com/rage-v.pdf

Rohlfs, Chris. *Does Military Service Make You a More Violent Person? Evidence from the Pre-Lottery Vietnam Draft and the Vietnam Draft Lottery*. Syracuse, NY: Syracuse University Center for Policy Research, November 2006. http://people.ucsc.edu/~cdobkin/Classes/Reza/Does%20Military%20Service%20Make%20You%20a%20More%20Violent%20Person.pdf

Springer, Nathan R. *Patterns of Radicalization: Identifying the Markers and Warning Signs of Domestic Lone Wolf Terrorists in Our Midst*. Graduate thesis. Monterey, CA: Naval Postgraduate School, December 2009. http://www.dtic.mil/cgi-bin/GetTRDoc?Location=U2&doc=GetTRDoc.pdf&AD=ADA514419

Threat Assessment Team Guide. Washington, DC: United States Postal Service, May 1997. http://www.postalreporter.com/usps/manuals/pub108.pdf

Wagoner, Larry. "Predicting Violent Behavior Among Inmates: Washington Correctional Institute's Development of a Risk Protection Tool." *Corrections Today* Vol. 66 No. 6 (2004). http://www.thefreelibrary.com/Predicting+violent+behavior+among+inmates%3A+Washington+Correctional...-a0123670338

Suicide

Shelby, Edward A., et al. "Overcoming the Fear of Lethal Injury: Evaluating Suicidal Behavior in the Military through the Lens of the Interpersonal-Psychological Theory of Suicide." *Clinical Psychology Review* No. 30 (2010): 298-307. http://www.wjh.harvard.edu/~nock/nocklab/Selby%20et%20al_ClinPsycRev_2010.pdf

Satel, Sally. "PTSD and Personality Disorders: Challenges for the VA." Testimony before the U.S. House of Representatives, Committee on Veterans' Affairs. Washington, DC: United States Congress, July 25, 2007. http://www.aei.org/speech/26542

Thompson, Mark. "A Soldier's Tragedy." *Time* (March 7, 2011). http://www.time.com/time/magazine/article/0,9171,2055169,00.html

Wood, David. "Combat Stress Driving Up Army Crime, Drug Abuse, Suicides." *Politics Daily* (October 17, 2010). http://www.politicsdaily.com/2010/10/17/combat-stress-driving-up-army-crime-drug-abuse-suicides/

Workplace and Campus Violence

Campus Attacks: Targeted Violence Affecting Institutions of Higher Learning. Washington, DC: U.S. Secret Service, Department of Education, and FBI, April 2010. http://www2.ed.gov/admins/lead/safety/campus-attacks.pdf

Dealing with Workplace Violence: A Guide for Agency Planners. Washington, DC: U.S. Office of Personnel Management, February 1998. http://www.opm.gov/employment_and_benefits/worklife/officialdocuments/handbooksguides/workplaceviolence/full.pdf

Fein, Robert A., et al. *The Final Report and Findings of the Safe School Initiative: Implications for the Prevention of School Attacks in the United States*. Washington, DC: United States

Secret Service and United States Department of Education, May 2002.
http://www.secretservice.gov/ntac/ssi_final_report.pdf

Gallagher, Robert P. *National Survey of Counseling Center Directors 2009*. Alexandria, VA:
International Association of Counseling Services and The American College Counseling
Association, 2009. http://www.iacsinc.org/2009%20National%20Survey.pdf

"Managing High-Risk Employees: A Review of *Aggression in the Workplace: Preventing and
Managing High-Risk Behavior*." *Risk Management Magazine* (March 2006): 6.

Mass Shootings at Virginia Tech: Addendum to the Report of the Review Panel. Arlington, VA:
TriData Division, System Planning Corporation, November 2009.
http://www.governor.virginia.gov/tempcontent/techPanelReport-
docs/VT_Addendum_12-2-2009.pdf

Mass Shootings at Virginia Tech: Report of the Review Panel. Arlington, VA: TriData Division,
System Planning Corporation, August 2007.
http://scholar.lib.vt.edu/prevail/docs/April16ReportRev20100106.pdf

Messmer, Ellen. "Can You No Longer Avoid Closely Monitoring Employees? Insider Threat Said
to be Increasing IT Security Risk in Tough Economic Times." *Network World* (April 27,
2009). http://www.networkworld.com/news/2009/042709-burning-security-insider-
threat.html

*National Association of Attorneys General Task Force on School and Campus Safety – Report
and Recommendations*. Washington, DC: National Association of Attorneys General,
September 2007. http://www.ago.state.ms.us/images/uploads/forms/NAAG-
SchoolSafety.pdf

Pollack, William S., et al. *Prior Knowledge of Potential School-Based Violence: Information
Students Learn May Prevent a Targeted Attack*. Washington, DC: United States Secret
Service and Department of Education, May 2008.
http://www.secretservice.gov/ntac/bystander_study.pdf

Promoting Mental Health and Preventing Suicide in College and University Settings. Newton,
MA: Education Development Center, Inc., 2004.
http://www.sprc.org/library/college_sp_whitepaper.pdf

Schaefer-Schiumo, Kristin and Amy Patraka Ginsberg. "The Effectiveness of the Warning Signs
Program in Educating Youth about Violence Prevention: A Study With Urban High School
Students." *Professional School Counseling* Vol. 7 No. 1 (October 2003): 1-8.
http://www.schoolcounselor.org/files/7-1-1%20Schaefer.pdf

Stock, Harley V. "Workplace Violence: Advances in Consultation and Assessment." In Goldstein,
Alan M., ed., *Forensic Psychology: Emerging Topics and Expanding Roles*. Hoboken, NJ:

John Wiley & Sons, 2007: 511-550.
http://books.google.com/books/about/Forensic_psychology.html?id=uRrTSounS7IC

Thrower, Raymond H., et al. *Overview of the Virginia Tech Tragedy and Implications for Campus Safety: The IACLEA Blueprint for Safer Campuses*. West Hartford, CT: International Association of Campus Law Enforcement Administrators, April 2008. http://www.iaclea.org/visitors/PDFs/VT-taskforce-report_Virginia-Tech.pdf

Mass Murder

Klofas, John. "Summary of Research on Mass Murder." Working Paper #125. Rochester, NY: Center for Public Safety Initiatives, Rochester Institute of Technology, May 2009. http://www.rit.edu/cla/cpsi/WorkingPapers/2009/2009-11.pdf

Targeted Violence

Protecting Judicial Officials: Implementing an Effective Threat Management Process. Washington, DC: U.S. Department of Justice, Office of Justice Programs, June 2006. http://www.ncjrs.gov/pdffiles1/bja/213930.pdf

Privacy/HIPAA

Balancing Student Privacy and School Safety: A Guide to the Family Educational Rights and Privacy Act for Colleges and Universities. Washington, DC: U.S. Department of Education, undated. http://www2.ed.gov/policy/gen/guid/fpco/brochures/postsec.pdf

Conti, Gregory, et al. "The Military's Cultural Disregard for Personal Information." *Small Wars Journal* (December 6, 2010). http://smallwarsjournal.com/blog/journal/docs-temp/615-conti.pdf

Health Insurance Portability and Accountability Act of 1996 – Conference Report. Washington, DC: United States Congress, House of Representatives, 104th Congress 2nd Session, July 1996. http://www.gpo.gov/fdsys/pkg/CRPT-104hrpt736/pdf/CRPT-104hrpt736.pdf

Student Mental Health and the Law: A Resource for Institutions of Higher Education. New York, NY: The Jed Foundation, 2008. http://www.jedfoundation.org/assets/Programs/Program_downloads/StudentMentalHealth_Law_2008.pdf

Summary of the HIPAA Privacy Rule. Washington, DC: United States Department of Health and Human Services, May 2003. http://www.hhs.gov/ocr/privacy/hipaa/understanding/summary/privacysummary.pdf

The Privacy Act of 1974. U.S. Code. Vol. 5, sec. 552a (1974). http://www.justice.gov/opcl/privstat.htm

Zoroya, Gregg. "Is Army's Anti-Suicide Effort An Invasion?" *USA Today* (April 1, 2011). http://www.usatoday.com/printedition/news/20110401/suicides01_st.art.htm

Insider Threat

Behavioral Science Guidelines for Assessing Insider Threats. Lincoln, NE: University of Nebraska Public Policy Center, July 2008. http://ppc.nebraska.edu/userfiles/file/Documents/projects/ThreatAssessment/BehavSci enceGuidelinesforInsiderThreat.pdf

Brackney, Richard C. and Robert H. Anderson. "Understanding the Insider Threat: Proceedings of a March 2004 Workshop." Santa Monica, CA: The RAND Corporation, 2004. http://www.rand.org/pubs/conf_proceedings/2005/RAND_CF196.pdf

Catrantzos, Nick. "No Dark Corners: A Different Answer to Insider Threats." *Homeland Security Affairs* Vol. 1 No. 2 (Mary 2010): 1-20. http://dodreports.com/pdf/ada508935.pdf

Crescenzi, Anthony and Jeffrey Isherwood. "Mitigating Insider Threat Within Correctional Facilities." *Corrections Today* (December 2006): 88-89.

Responsible Research with Biological Select Agents and Toxins. Washington, DC: National Academies Press/National Research Council Committee on Laboratory Security and Personnel Reliability Assurance Systems for laboratories Conducting Research on Biological Select Agents and Toxins, 2009. http://www.ncbi.nlm.nih.gov/books/NBK44956/pdf/TOC.pdf

Strohm, Chris. "Panel Sees Mounting Bioterror Risk." *Congress Daily PM* (September 22, 2009). http://www.govexec.com/dailyfed/0909/092209cdpm1.htm

Department of Defense Reports

2008 Department of Defense Survey of Health Related Behaviors Among Active Duty Military Personnel. Washington, DC: Department of Defense, September 2009. http://www.tricare.mil/2008HealthBehaviors.pdf

Army Health Promotion, Risk Reduction, Suicide Prevention Report 2010. Washington, DC: United States Army, 2010. http://csf.army.mil/downloads/HP-RR-SPReport2010.pdf

DoD Directive 6490.1 "Mental Health Evaluations of Members of the Armed Forces." Washington, DC: Department of Defense, November 24, 2003. http://www.dodig.mil/hotline/Documents/DODInstructions/DOD%20Directive%206490.1.pdf

Flyer, Eli. *Reducing the Threat of Destructive Behavior by Military Personnel.* Washington, DC: Deputy Assistant Secretary of Defense for Military Personnel Policy, September 2003. http://dvmx.com/Flyer_Report.pdf

Protecting the Force: Lessons from Fort Hood – Report of the DoD Independent Review. Washington, DC: Department of Defense, January 2010. http://www.defense.gov/pubs/pdfs/DOD-ProtectingTheForce-Web_Security_HR_13jan10.pdf

The Challenge and the Promise: Strengthening the Force, Preventing Suicide, and Saving Lives – Final Report of the Department of Defense Task Force on the Prevention of Suicide by Members of the Armed Forces. Washington, DC: Department of Defense, August 2010. http://www.health.mil/dhb/downloads/Suicide%20Prevention%20Task%20Force%20fin al%20report%208-23-10.pdf

Department of Justice and FBI Reports

Band, Stephen R. and Joseph A. Harpold. "School Violence: Lessons Learned." *FBI Law Enforcement Bulletin* (September 1999). http://findarticles.com/p/articles/mi_m2194/is_9_68/ai_56750210/

O'Toole, Mary Ellen. *The School Shooter: A Threat Assessment Perspective.* Quantico, VA: FBI Academy CIRG/NCAVC, undated. http://www.fbi.gov/stats-services/publications/school-shooter

Report to the President on Issues Raised by the Virginia Tech Tragedy. Washington, DC: DoJ, DoE, and HHS, June 13, 2007. http://www.hsdl.org/?view&doc=77584&coll=limited

The School Shooter: A Quick Reference Guide. Washington, DC: DoJ/FBI, 1999. https://www6.miami.edu/public-safety/Emergency_Preparedness_Webpage/FBI-School_Shooter_Quick_Reference_Guide.pdf

Newsmedia

Batdorff, Allison and Hana Kusumoto. "Navy Watching for Sailors Prone to Violent Behavior." *Stars and Stripes* (May 3, 2008). http://www.stripes.com/news/navy-watching-for-sailors-prone-to-violent-behavior-1.78373

McKinley, James C. Jr. "Despite Army Efforts, Soldier Suicides Continue." *The New York Times* (October 10, 2010). http://www.nytimes.com/2010/10/11/us/11suicides.html

Peters, Katherine McIntire. "Dark Hour: After Nine Years of War, the Army is Grappling with Growing Rates of Suicide, Crime, and Drug Abuse in the Ranks." *Government Executive* (October 1, 2010). http://www.govexec.com/features/1010-01/1010-01s2.htm

Pincus, Walter. "Inquiry into Fort Hood Shootings Urges New Programs to Identify Violent Behavior." *The Washington Post* (January 19, 2010): A15. http://www.washingtonpost.com/wp-dyn/content/article/2010/01/18/AR2010011803520.html

Silverstein, Ken. "Pentagon Alerted to Trouble in Ranks: Reports over a decade have warned of recruits with criminal pasts and of the violent behavior of some active-duty service members." *The Los Angeles Times* (July 1, 2004). http://articles.latimes.com/2004/jul/01/nation/na-violent1

Sluss, Michael. "Governor Signs Virginia Tech-inspired Mental Health Reform Bills." *The Roanoke Times* (April 9, 2009). http://www.roanoke.com/news/breaking/wb/157560

NTAC Insider Threat Study

Keeney, Michelle, et al. *Insider Threat Study; Computer System Sabotage in Critical Infrastructure Sectors*. Washington, DC: United States Secret Service and Carnegie Mellon Software Engineering Institute, May 2005. www.cert.org/archive/pdf/insidercross051105.pdf

Kowalski, Eileen, et al. *Insider Threat Study: Illicit Cyber Activity in the Government Sector*. Washington, DC: United States Secret Service and Carnegie Mellon Software Engineering Institute, January 2008. http://www.secretservice.gov/ntac/gov%20ExecSummary%202008_0108.pdf

_____. *Insider Threat Study: Illicit Cyber Activity in the Information Technology and Telecommunications Sector*. Washington, DC: United States Secret Service and Carnegie Mellon Software Engineering Institute, January 2008. www.cert.org/archive/pdf/insiderthreat_it2008.pdf

Randazzo, Marisa, et al. *Insider Threat Study: Illicit Cyber Activity in the Banking and Finance Sector*. Washington, DC: United States Secret Service and Carnegie Mellon Software Engineering Institute, August 2004. http://www.sei.cmu.edu/reports/04tr021.pdf

NTAC Safe School Initiative

Fein, Robert A. et al., *Threat Assessment in Schools: A Guide to Managing Threatening Situations and to Creating Safe School Climates*. Washington, DC: USSS and Department of Education, May 2002. http://www.secretservice.gov/ntac/ssi_guide.pdf

Reddy, Marisa, et al. "Evaluating Risk for Targeted Violence in Schools: Comparing Risk Assessment, Threat Assessment, and Other Approaches." *Psychology in the Schools* Vol. 38 No. 2 (2001): 157-172. http://www.secretservice.gov/ntac/ntac_threat_postpress.pdf

Vossekuil, Bryan, et al. *The Final Report and Findings of the Safe School Initiative: Implications for the Prevention of School Attacks in the United States*. Washington, DC: USSS and Department of Education, May 2002. http://www.secretservice.gov/ntac/ssi_final_report.pdf

USSS Exceptional Case Study Project

Borum, Randy, et al. "Threat Assessment: Defining an Approach for Evaluating Risk of Targeted Violence." *Behavioral Sciences and the Law* Vol. 17 (1999): 323-337. http://www.secretservice.gov/ntac/ntac_bsl99.pdf

Fein, Robert A. and Bryan Vasserkuil. "Assassination in the United States: An Operation Study of Recent Assassins, Attackers, and Near-Lethal Approachers." *Journal of Forensic Sciences* Vol. 44 No. 2 (March 1999). http://www.secretservice.gov/ntac/ntac_jfs.pdf

_____. *Protective Intelligence and Threat Assessment Investigations: A Guide for State and Local Law Enforcement Officials*. Washington, DC: Department of Justice, July 1998. http://www.secretservice.gov/ntac/PI_Guide.pdf

_____. "Threat Assessment: An Approach to Targeted Violence." *Research in Action – National Institute of Justice* (July 1995). http://www.secretservice.gov/ntac/ntac_threat.pdf

START Reports

Ackerman, Gary A. and John P. Sawyer. *Islamic Radicalization in Europe and North America: Parallels and Divergences*. Washington, DC: National Consortium for the Study of Terrorism and Responses to Terrorism, August 2010.

Blair, Charles P. and Gary A. Ackerman. *Anatomizing Radiological and Nuclear Non-State Adversaries – Executive Summary*. Washington, DC: National Consortium for the Study of Terrorism and Responses to Terrorism, October 2009.

Fishman, Shira. *Community-Level Indicators of Radicalization – Final Report*. Washington, DC: National Consortium for the Study of Terrorism and Responses to Terrorism, February 2010.